CHIVALRY AND COURTESY

Danièle Cybulskie

Illustrations by Anna Lobanova

CHIVALRY
AND
COURTESY

Medieval Manners
For A Modern World

ABBEVILLE PRESS
New York   London

To my parents, who taught me the magic words. —Danièle Cybulskie

Editor: Lauren Orthey
Copy Editor: Ashley Benning
Design: Misha Beletsky and Marina Drukman
Production: Louise Kurtz
Indexer: Cathy Dorsey

First edition
1 3 5 7 9 10 8 6 4 2

Library of Congress Cataloging-in-Publication Data
Names: Cybulskie, Danièle, author.
Title: Chivalry and courtesy : medieval manners for a modern world / Danièle Cybulskie. Description: First edition. | New York : Abbeville Press, 2023. | Includes bibliographical references and index. | Summary: "An illustrated book on the lessons of medieval etiquette for today"— Provided by publisher. Identifiers: LCCN 2023023292 | ISBN 9780789214690 (hardcover) Subjects: LCSH: Chivalry. | Courtesy. | Etiquette. Classification: LCC CR4515 .C94 2023 | DDC 390.09/02—dc23/eng/20230602
LC record available at https://lccn.loc.gov/2023023292

For bulk and premium sales and for text adoption procedures, write to Customer Service Manager, Abbeville Press, 655 Third Avenue, New York, NY 10017, or call 1-800-Artbook.

Visit Abbeville Press online at www.abbeville.com.

The Five-Minute Medievalist logo by Eric Overton

Contents

INTRODUCTION

If you, dear reader, want to be polished with morals and
   manners,
if you want the esteem of worthy men, or want to lead a
   civilised life among noble lords, to be a shrewd observer
   of your property, keep these everlasting verses in mind,
which I have decided to write
   in unadorned plain speech for untrained boy-clerks.
      —Daniel of Beccles, *The Book of the Civilised Man*

O n the surface, writing a book on medieval manners might seem like a very short project. After all, many modern people consider the very definition of *medieval* as uncouth, uncivilized, and unclean. In reality, hundreds of books surviving from the Middle Ages (the period between roughly 500 and 1500) focus on good manners, polite etiquette, and fair governance.

To understand medieval chivalry and courtesy in their own context, it's worth taking a moment to get a sense of the society we're about to encounter. This book focuses on Western Europe, mainly England and France, during what historians call the High and Late Middle Ages. Rather than concerning ourselves with earlier societies like those of the Vikings—who themselves were deeply image-conscious—we'll be looking at the period from about the twelfth century on, when ideals of courtly love and chivalry in the forms that are familiar today began to take shape and be written down.

In this time and place, social status was mainly fixed, with the majority of people being the peasants who performed agricultural work, while above them were artisans, tradespeople, and low-level government in the form of sheriffs, town councillors, or mayors. Above these sat the aristocracy: landowners born to privileged families and usually wealth. At the very top was the royal family, with the king at its head. Interwoven within all ranks of society were the clergy, ranging in influence from the limited local authority of parish priests to the landowning privilege of abbots and abbesses to the coronating powers of archbishops. Technically, popes ruled over kings in both temporal and spiritual power, but this was not something kings liked to think about on a daily basis.

However, social class in medieval Europe was not as static as either modern people or medieval people may have wished. At every level, it was complicated by other factors, such as gender, religion, education, and of course, wealth. Men were considered above women, with young women and wives having less power than widows. Christians sat above Jews and Muslims in Christian states, while Muslims sat above Christians and Jews in Muslim states. Educated peasants could be elevated to the heart of government through appointments within the church, and a wealthy merchant could ennoble his family through a strategic marriage with an aristocratic family in need of cash. Physical attractiveness—with blonde hair and fair skin perceived as the height of beauty—influenced the opportunities available to both men and women. Then there were those random moments of fate, when an ordinary man could be knighted in battle, a woman of great skill could become an adviser to princes, and a royal family member could be brought down by scandal and executed for treason. There was a reason why the Wheel of Fortune was one of medieval Europe's most popular memes.

The Wheel of Fortune was a popular image in medieval art, warning against the capriciousness of Lady Luck, who spares no one a fall.

L'Épître Othéa, fol. 129r, c. 1410–14 (detail)
British Library, London; Harley 4431

Figuring out where someone sat on the social ladder might be a confusing tangle for us at this distance, but it was immediately evident to those within medieval society itself—and a determining factor was manners. One contemporary author wrote,

> Learned men say that the greatest part of good fortune is given to a man enriched with the grace of manners. Nothing in the world will be a surer help to you than proper manners.[1]

A person's status was understood at first glance by the clothes they wore, the words they used, and the way they comported themselves in social situations. Manners were, as this author implies, a way to make an end run around privilege and give yourself a leg up in the world.

In the twelfth century, people began writing books of manners which consolidated the ideas of chivalry and courtesy—especially courtly love—the way we understand them today: as acts of polite behavior, especially as they might apply to the "opposite sex."[2] These books were almost exclusively addressed to the middle and upper classes, since they were the ones who could both read and afford them. Although women tended to be the ones who taught their children both their letters and manners at an early age, most books of manners were not written by women. Instead, these books of courtesy were composed by educated men, often clergy, who tended to be nobles themselves. Books that addressed the highest circles, called "mirrors for princes," were written or compiled by those who had enough status—or audacity—to dare address royals directly.

For these reasons, in this book we'll mainly look at the advice given to people above the rank of peasant. This doesn't mean that peasants were mannerless, of course;

only that the hierarchy of literacy in the Middle Ages makes it very difficult to access their thoughts on etiquette, given that their wisdom and advice would mainly have been passed on orally and by example. It's overwhelmingly likely that medieval peasants had much better manners than modern society gives them credit for. After all, it's always been a good survival strategy to endear yourself to those around you, and being unkind or eating like an animal is unlikely to impress people in any historical era.

At their core, both chivalry and courtesy are meant to be about respect. Both imply molding our behavior to treat others well and often to place their needs above our own, whether that means serving them first at the table or as a champion in arms. Both also imply that kindness should be extended to those less fortunate. These are worthy ideals. When it comes to creating rules around both courtesy and chivalry, however, boundaries for things like social class, lineage, and wealth begin to appear. A person who is going to ridicule someone else for not using the correct fork is someone who is overly concerned with the trees, as it were, not the forest.

This book is mainly focused on the trees; namely, those rules that medieval people were meant to follow in order to gain prestige or status within the confines of their society. Along the way, we'll also explore the forest—that is, what we can learn from medieval history that will help us to live fuller lives without being pinned down to specific or outdated rules.

Before we begin, it's important to take a moment to recognize that societal standards for how to act, react, dress, and comport ourselves can sometimes feel unkind and restrictive. It's best to remember that while these standards may exist as cultural expectations, kindness will always take us much further than choosing the right fork. After all, rules are made to be broken.

HOW TO EAT

This is the inarguable rule for hosts:
   a stern look that betrays unhappiness overshadows
   your elegant table.
A generous hand with your food gives you a sumptuous
   reputation.
      —Daniel of Beccles, *The Book of the Civilised Man*

For the people of medieval Europe, to share food was to create a bond of peace and trust between diners, if only for the span of a meal. Hearkening back to the Eucharist—the heart of the Christian mass in which Jesus's body and blood are shared with believers—providing guests with bread and wine, staples at a medieval table, was deeply meaningful and symbolic. It was a way of showing goodwill, generosity, and hospitality. At the same time, meals could also be raucous and joyful events, especially when accompanied by entertainment.

As an activity so central to life and social relationships, eating at table was the perfect place to show off your impeccable manners as a polite member of society, regardless of your social rank.

Set the Stage

Invited guests were to arrive at medieval feasts on time and to send their apologies if they could not be there. The truly posh were to be selective about which dinners they attended, since, as twelfth-century etiquette writer Daniel of Beccles suggests, "people hold rare things more precious."[1] Because the most important meals were served in the great hall of a house or castle, it might be tempting to make a dramatic entrance, but Daniel advises, "When you enter, do not have your head covered, do not have a sword at your side, / and do not enter on horseback, unless you are pressed to."[2]

Upon arriving at a wealthy medieval home, guests would be greeted by servants who would gently pour water over their hands, so they could wash before eating. Ewers called aquamaniles or decorated pairs of bowls called gemellions turned this ritual into a moment of beauty—and sometimes humor—as water flowed from the mouths of fantastic creatures. The water might be lightly scented with flower petals, although no soap would be offered; soap was for baths, not handwashing. After each guest wiped their hands on the linen towel provided, they would be shown to their seat by an usher. Along the way, and between exchanging greetings with their fellow diners, guests were meant to notice and be impressed by the garlands and tapestries hung around the hall, freshened and displayed specially for the occasion.

Because a great hall was a multipurpose room, people used trestle tables—long boards which sat on structures

Handwashing provided an opportunity to showcase fancy ewers, like this aquamanile (from the Latin for "water" and "hands") of a mounted knight.
Aquamanile, c. 1250
The Met Cloisters, New York

To elevate the handwashing ritual, servants might pour water from one basin (gemellion) to another via a decorative spout in the shape of an animal or gargoyle, like this one.
Gemellion, c. 1250–75
The Met Cloisters, New York

similar to sawhorses—which were easy to set up and take down. Most of the people who attended a feast would be seated on long benches facing inward, while the host, hostess, and especially chosen guests sat at their own table on a slightly raised platform called a dais. This formal configuration of important figures at a high table and lesser guests sitting down the hall (with the least significant guests closest to the exit) is a familiar one, still seen at weddings, banquets, and other formal occasions. Seating plans continue to require a fine balance between tradition, politics, emotional intelligence, and tact.

A well-laid table in the Middle Ages included a clean, white linen tablecloth of the best quality the host could afford. "One can have a meal without a table," says Daniel of Beccles, "but not without a tablecloth."[3] As a vital decorative element, the tablecloth was there to make the meal elegant, so it was rude to splatter it with sauce or grease while serving or eating. Well-mannered guests were never to wipe their hands, food, or teeth on it, but

Even outside, a well-laid table included a tablecloth.
Arthurian Romances, fol. 31r, c. 1290–1300 (detail)
Yale University Library, New Haven, CT; Beineke 229

on the linen napkins provided. If a host or hostess did not have enough table linens on hand to suit the event, these could be rented out for the day, along with extra dishes and pots.[4]

Once the tablecloth was in place, the table would be laid with the household's finest dishes of silver, gold, pewter, pottery, horn, or wood. Plates—or trenchers—could be fashioned from any of these materials, but they were frequently made of stale bread. The Goodman of Paris, a wealthy French citizen of the fifteenth century, instructs that a servant go to the baker's and buy "brown trencher breads, half a foot long and 4 fingers wide and high, baked 4 days before" in addition to the "flat white loaves baked the day before," which were for eating.[5] Although the relative surface area of trenchers may seem small in comparison to today's dinner plates, they accommodated two diners each, even at the high table.

Goblets or cups were likewise shared by two people, and were often even more expensive than plates, made of

Hanaps were one of several options for medieval drinkers. In this one, a half-man/half-beast appears in the bottom as the wine is drunk.

Drinking vessel (hanap; one of a pair), c. 1320–60
The Met Cloisters, New York

Mazers were drinking bowls made of maple burls or coconut shells, decorated with precious metals.

Drinking bowl, 1450–99
The Met Cloisters, New York

precious metal, bejeweled and etched, or even fashioned from blown glass. Hanaps, or drinking bowls or cups, were to be provided in addition to "covered golden goblets" for at least one Parisian wedding, while special cups made of carved maple or coconut shells, called mazers, were often used further down the social chain to toast or to seal agreements.[6] If a host didn't have enough precious cups for everyone, or feared they'd be stolen, wooden or clay cups would suffice for the lower tables.

A saltcellar was an essential item on any medieval table, both for seasoning and as a symbol of generosity. While salt wasn't exclusive to the wealthy, it was still relatively expensive, so saltcellars were often dramatic, eye-catching works of art that showed off the household's wealth and good taste—both aesthetically and literally. As a result, the people with the highest status sat within reach of the saltcellar, or "above the salt." Lesser guests were seated "below the salt," or farther away. Because it would be ungenerous to deprive the lower tables of salt completely, servants provided mini saltcellars made out of bread.[7]

Although you wouldn't find a butler with a measuring stick placing tableware as you might expect in the nineteenth century, medieval people were still sticklers for making sure the table was laid properly with correctly oriented utensils and spotless dishes. Daniel of Beccles's *Book of the Civilised Man*, a treatise meant to instruct boys who might become servants as well as those who might serve at table as part of their knightly training, provides detailed instructions, including how to place the knives when setting up: "The knives' handles should face the diners when they are set down [and] should not be blocking the salt cellar."[8]

Incidentally, butlers could still be found at medieval feasts: their job was to make sure that everyone was adequately supplied with wine from the host's barrels or "butts." They also ensured that the drinking cups, saltcellar, and dishes were prepared and placed for the VIPs at the top table. A pantler (from the French *pain*, meaning "bread") made sure that every guest had enough bread, something kept in the pantry.[9] Butlers, pantlers, servants, and most kitchen staff were men.[10]

Once dishes, cups, knives, spoons, napkins, and the saltcellar were added, the whole table arrangement would be elevated with the addition of cut flowers and greenery, either picked up early by a servant or provided (like the garlands) by a florist on the day of the event.[11]

When all the guests had been shown their seats amid the rising cacophony of music and small talk, it was time for the meal to begin.

Setting the table prettily is still seen as a sign

This ornate saltcellar would have been used by the most distinguished banquet guests.
Saltcellar, c. 1250
The Met Cloisters, New York

*This scene shows the essentials of medieval dining: a
tablecloth, plates, tiny saltcellars, and eating knives.*
Simon Marmion (active 1450–89), *Les Visions du chevalier
Tondal*, fol. 7r, 1475 (detail)
Getty Museum, Los Angeles; MS 30

of respect for guests, as it shows thoughtfulness and time
spent on preparation. While having elaborate sets of expensive dishes has fallen somewhat out of fashion, good
hosts still strive to provide everything a guest may need,
including salt and napkins, and we still dress our fanciest
tables with flowers and candles.

If your budget doesn't allow for expensive table settings, no problem. As Daniel says, "A spotless tablecloth,
even if threadbare, will be enough to dress the table."[12]
Hosting itself is a generous act, and the best guests know
that thoughtfulness is more important than fine linen.

Choose Your Weapon

S itting down at a formal table today, an uninitiated guest might look nervously at the wide range of cutlery set before them, each with its own specific function and designated dish. In the Middle Ages, however, people used fewer utensils, and they did eat with their hands. Luckily, handwashing was an important part of medieval culture, as we've seen. *The Boke of Curtasye* goes so far as to say, "With hondes unwasshen take never thy mete,"[13] and Daniel of Beccles even provides a contingency plan to ensure hands are washed: "If there are no basins, cups will serve for rinsing your fingers."[14]

Although the idea of consuming food like chicken with your hands sounds exotic when used as a hook for a medieval-themed restaurant, we still eat this way on the regular; even at modern restaurants, no one is expected to eat chicken wings with a knife and fork. Medieval rules for eating with your hands politely will sound familiar to anyone who's ever shared an appetizer: "Pick food up courteously with your index finger and thumb [and d]o not stoop to licking your greasy fingers." Everyone was expected to use their napkins to clean their hands and faces throughout the meal, which kept the communal dishes a little cleaner, too. To help with this, and to avoid any social awkwardness, "Dinner companions should not reach their fingers into a dish at the same time."[15] Fortunately, most dishes were served with spoons.

Sometimes used as expensive and elaborate gifts, spoons could be status symbols, as well as tempting targets for thieves.
Spoon, 15th century
The Met Cloisters, New York

While we may not pay much attention to our spoons these days, medieval spoons were used at many, if not most meals, for eating as well as serving and stirring food. Spoons could be sentimental objects, given to people on special occasions such as weddings or baptisms, and often had great monetary value.[16] As a result, it might have been tempting to steal the fancy spoon provided for you at table, but of course, this was a terrible breach of etiquette, as well as being a violation of the rules of hospitality.[17] Daniel of Beccles lays out several other important rules for spoons meant to keep both diners and tablecloths looking polished and clean:

> The spoons should not rest next to the dish
>   and do not burden them with oversized mouthfuls,
>   or you risk a morsel falling off.
> When you pick up food with a spoon, do not shovel it
>   on board with your thumb. . . .
> After taking food from the serving dishes, wipe the
>   spoons clean with your napkin.[18]

At some medieval-themed restaurants, spoons are not provided—even for soup—in order to keep the experience "authentic." However, medieval diners considered it impolite to "pick up your dish to gulp down your sauces," as well as to mop up any remaining sauce or soup with either fingers or bread.[19]

The other indispensable utensil was a knife, which was designated for individual carving or stirring—it was not meant to be the same knife that was used for combat. While a host might supply spoons or knives at a feast, people often carried their own knives with them in sheaths on their belts.[20] Despite what we might see in the movies, it was considered impolite to eat off your knife or to toss it down on the table and mess up the tablecloth.

Knives were ubiquitous in the Middle Ages,
especially those for eating, like this one, which
says, "S'il plait a Dieu" ("If it is pleasing to God").
Knife, c. 1406
British Museum, London

Tableware could be extremely decorative, as with this
serving knife which reads on one side, "The blessing
of the table. May the three-in-one bless that which
we are about to eat," and on the other, "The saying of
grace. We give thanks to you God for your generosity,"
with accompanying musical notation to guide singers.
Serving knife, c. 1550
Victoria and Albert Museum, London

If you happen to find yourself with a messy knife these days, remember: "Do not lick [it] or wipe it on your stirred eggs. / Wipe your knife with bread and set it back on the table."[21] Although you might dip your knife into a dish to stir something, it must never be dipped in the salt-cellar. Instead, take a pinch with your fingers, and you'll avoid offending your host and spilling expensive salt on the table.[22]

While people were meant to use their hands to "tear fresh hare, lamb, rabbit, and pork . . . any meat that is formed into a loaf should be cut," says Daniel, and "whale, seal and porpoise meat should be carved up."[23] Carving was meant to be done "elegantly . . . in one fluid motion," just one of the many ways in which medieval people could show off their refinement, as well as the fine quality of their knives.

Navigating utensils at formal dinners today can seem a little tricky at the outset, just as it must have for medieval people who found themselves unexpectedly eating with their social superiors. Luckily, we can always watch those with the fanciest manners and emulate them in the moment. But whether at a dinner centuries ago or one up to the minute, you can't go wrong with these simple medieval tips: don't mess up the linens, don't overload your spoon, and definitely don't put anything you've licked back into a communal dish.

Dig In

As bread was a ubiquitous food at a medieval table, the way a person ate it was one of the first places to sink or swim in terms of manners. White bread, finely milled, was served to the most important people at a medieval feast, with the bread getting darker and coarser as it was passed down the lower ranks. Loaves of bread were meant to be cut or torn with the hands, not bitten into directly, and we can still see people following this rule today in formal settings. When cutting, "do not use lethal force against your bread," but slice it smoothly into two or four pieces, never three. And once you've bitten in, remember to follow the cardinal rule and never, ever double-dip.[24]

Trenchers made of bread made handy plates, as they soaked up grease from meat and sauce from other dishes, but actually eating your trencher was a sign of ill breeding, not to mention tough going, given that it would be four days' stale. At the end of the feast, servants would be sent around with baskets to collect trenchers and leftovers to give to the poor.

At a medieval-style feast today, you might be served soup, a main course, and dessert, but actual medieval feasts featured more courses, with some of the food being entertainment in itself. Presentation was an essential part of formal dining, and even simple dishes were garnished and colored. Saffron gave pottages and puddings a bright golden hue. Sprigs of herbs provided a pop of green. Fowl

A common theme in medieval art, the Castle of Love illustrates the chivalrous ideal of men laying siege to capture women's affections, and women putting up a token resistance.
Roundel, c. 1320–40
The Met Cloisters, New York

like swans and peacocks were often dressed again in their feathers and posed to look as though alive. Imaginative culinary inventions combined several different roasted animals to create mythical—and delicious—hybrid creatures, like the cockatrice. At one feast, individual pies were created to honor wedding guests with the heraldic symbols of each guest painted onto the crust with many of the same bright, plant-based pigments used to illuminate manuscripts.[25]

While these ordinary dishes were dressed to impress, *sotelties* or *entremets* were the pièce de résistance. Sotelties were carefully crafted, often immense, edible sculptures, served between courses or as dessert. Castles of love, complete with musicians, live birds bursting out of pies, cookies in the shape of biblical stories, and portraits made of marzipan were just some of the incredible works of art created by medieval culinary masters.

As the artistry that went into these presentations attests, each dish at a medieval feast was the result of thoughtful preparation, signaling not only good taste, but also political savvy and even the education of the host. Eating—then as now—was tied to health, so that consuming the right foods in the right amount was virtuous in both spiritual and physical ways. A well-mannered, well-educated host would provide a meal that opened the stomach, balanced

*Wine was such an essential part of medieval culture
that making it often appears as a symbol of the changing
seasons, as on this calendar page for September.*
Book of hours, fol. 9r, c. 1450–55 (detail)
Getty Museum, Los Angeles; MS 2

the humors, and closed the stomach, so that each guest
would end the meal healthier than when they arrived.

Given the care, thought, and expense that went into creating such a meal, it was exceptionally rude to criticize it or
to ask for something else. Luckily, with so many courses,
it was likely that there would be something you enjoyed
at several points during the meal. When such a moment
came, however, it was considered uncouth to take more
than your portion, no matter how good the food was. Gluttony, as one of the seven deadly sins, was unbecoming and
spoke ill of a person's character. Excess was seen as a lack
of judgment and control, and never was this more evident
than in a person's consumption of alcohol.

Offering wine was often the first gesture of hospitality,
and it was to be given freely to invited guests, unexpected
visitors, and even lowly messengers. Although people did
drink water, wine, then as now, was associated with sophis-
tication, wealth, and generosity. Wine was used to celebrate, toast, and seal agreements between people, making

the sharing of it inherently a gesture of friendship. After all, to loosen your inhibitions in the company of another is to trust them with your safety, and often your secrets.

At a large adult event in today's world, alcohol is frequently served, whether as predinner drinks or a bottle of wine for the table, and medieval people had the same expectation. In the same way that modern guests may appreciate an open bar at a wedding, a well-stocked party in the Middle Ages meant that people would not only be talking later about the host's openhanded attitude toward food and drink, but also the quality of the food and drink themselves.

Drunkenness, depicted at the bottom table, was looked upon as both sinful and unsophisticated. The figures at the top table are showing the sober temperance of the well-mannered.

Faits et Dits Mémorables des Romains, miniature, recto, c. 1475–80 (detail)
Getty Museum, Los Angeles; MS 43

Drinking, of course, came with the danger of over-indulging, something that medieval people found by turns distasteful and par for the course. Getting drunk was sinful—evidence of gluttony made manifest. It was thought that a strong and rational person should be able to hold their drink without it making them messy, sloppy, or worse: lustful.

> Your speech, gestures, posture, and gait reveal your
> drunkenness.
> Show that you are a sensible man who is mindful of his
> reputation,
> and keep in mind the difference between your head
> and your genitals.[26]

Because women were thought to be innately irrational, lusty, and prone to sin, they were cautioned even more emphatically against drunkenness.[27]

At the same time, hosts were meant to keep plying their guests with alcohol in the spirit of generosity, so the virtuous had a very fine line to walk between drinking enough to prevent offending the host and yet not so much that they ended up drunk. It was inevitable that people sometimes slipped on one side or the other.

If you happen to overindulge, the best advice remains timeless: sleep it off. If you can't sleep, Daniel of Beccles says to at least remove yourself from the party and pretend to sleep—complete with snoring—so "you can bury the shame of your drunken behaviour better."[28]

Whatever the menu or the occasion, food and drink in the Middle Ages were expected to be tasty, well-presented, and plentiful, demonstrating the generosity, wealth, and hospitality of the host. As modern hosts, we may agree with our medieval counterparts that if we're going to trouble ourselves with nourishing and impressing our guests, the least they can do is be civilized.

Clean Up Your Act

F undamentally, good manners involve being respect-
ful and not grossing people out with bodily functions
or emissions. Although these rules applied to every social
situation in the medieval world—just as they do today—it
has always been especially important that people refrain
from being disgusting at mealtimes.

In *The Book of the Civilised Man*, Daniel of Beccles
sternly admonishes his readers against behaviors that
parents and teachers of young children will no doubt
find familiar:

> Do not be a boorish nose-blower or throat-clearer
>   while dining. If you need to cough, suppress that urge....
> If you empty your nose into your hand,
>   do not look at the filth on your palm....
> If you cannot use the back of your cloak, use the front
>   for cleaning yourself.[29]

Although adults in the medieval world often carried
linen handkerchiefs with them for such emergencies,
it was always important to have a backup plan. Modern
adults with the luxury of tissues may still wish to follow
Daniel's other advice: namely, "never clear your nose to-
wards [lords and ladies]." While on the topic of bodily
emissions, Daniel felt it necessary to address another familiar subject:

> Do not joke by letting rude noises slip suddenly....
> In public, your bottom should emit no secret winds
>   past your thighs.
> It disgraces you if others notice any of your smelly filth.
> If it happens that your intestines are caught in a
>   windstorm,
> look for a place where you may relieve them in private.[30]

It seems evident that, just like manners, jokes about flatulence are timeless, not to mention overwhelmingly tempting for children. For those who were ready for subtler maneuvers, Daniel adds, "If you feel the need to belch, remember to look at the ceiling."[31]

General manners related to the body also included not staring, scratching, looking for vermin, or picking your nose in front of people. "When you are alone," Daniel says, "your nails may have free rein."[32] Although medieval people have a reputation for being uncouth, attending to just about anything related to the body was not to be done in public:

> Remember not to remove your shoes, clean your feet,
>   wet your face, brush your long hairs,
> pare your nails, or shave your face
>   in the hall in front of great lords and ladies.[33]

Tempting as it might be, you should also not pick your teeth at the table with your knife, a piece of straw, or a stick. "If necessary," Daniel says, "rub them on a corner of your cloak to clean them, / so that nothing ugly can be seen lurking between your teeth."[34] If you're really stuck, you can excuse yourself and go pick your teeth with a handy-dandy toothpick-ear scoop of the kind uncovered by archaeologists.

This combination ear-spoon and toothpick shows concern for good grooming and hygiene, even if this particular solution may not appeal to us today.
Combined toothpick and ear-spoon, c. 1400–1700
Science Museum, London

Except for hunting vermin—an issue that hopefully most of us are not regularly afflicted with—all of these activities continue to be frowned upon in public. While good hygiene is important, keeping grooming behaviors private is still the baseline standard for manners upon which more sophisticated refinements can be made.

Beyond keeping things clean and not gross were layers of manners that we might call "politeness" instead of just basic human decency.[35] These rules of etiquette will be well-known to children and adults everywhere, and include sitting up straight, not putting your elbows on the table, not stealing from others' plates, and not talking with your mouth full:

> Do not sip your drink when you have food in your mouth,
> and do not talk when you have food in your mouth.
> A diner should not take so large a bite that he is completely unable to speak, if he were addressed.[36]

In a time before the Heimlich maneuver, taking small bites and chewing your food were not only polite things to do, but also potentially lifesaving habits.

The final layer of manners at the dinner table emphasized generosity and selflessness and has likewise remained timeless: when serving, make sure to give your dining partner the best out of the dish, saving the lesser portions for yourself.

Depictions of medieval feasts on the silver screen may make it seem as if table manners are one of the places where medieval and modern cultures are furthest apart, but in reality, the rules of basic etiquette are strikingly similar. Modern germ theory only emphasizes what we've always known: contaminating food with bodily fluids is not only off-putting but unhealthy, just as taking care of bodily functions in public is upsetting to other people. Eating in moderation is more polite than taking too much, while offering the best of everything to others is the height of gentility; indeed, it's expected from those of the highest social classes. Drinking alcohol is often considered (at least in Western cultures) as symbolic of trust, especially when it comes to sealing deals or celebrating, but drinking to excess is frowned upon as a sign of weakness.

Because eating together is still seen as a gesture of goodwill and an extension of friendship, this is perhaps the best way for us to practice refinement. Whether it's a business lunch, a wedding reception, or a UN summit, good table manners are often the gateway to good relationships, allowing us to make a positive impression on the people we want to impress most.

II
HOW ΤΟ WOO

No matter how you serve this love
It will pay you back a thousandfold.
To those who do it well
Come honor and joy and all[.]
                    —Cercamon, twelfth-century troubadour

hile love itself was not a priority in the aristocratic marriage market, taking a back seat to other factors such as wealth and property, it was still a many splen-dor'd thing; the subject of countless stories and songs. In the twelfth century arose a stylized idea of love called *fin' amors*, or courtly love, which became hugely influential in medieval culture and continues to impact our society today. Courtly love involved a man suffering greatly from an overwhelming passion and desire for a beautiful, unattainable lady he would swear to serve in all things. The rules for how to properly conduct such a romance are still found in many stories on page and screen—although we should definitely use caution when applying them to our own relationships.

Look Your Best

While beauty is not—and never has been—what makes a relationship successful, it was nonetheless a highly prized attribute when it came to courtly love. At a time when beauty was seen as both a blessing from God and an outward sign of inner virtue, even priests were meant to be handsome, despite their being completely off the marriage market.

Andreas Capellanus, author of the twelfth-century bestseller *The Art of Courtly Love*, explains that seeing someone beautiful is at the core of romance:

> Love is a certain inborn suffering derived from the sight of and excessive meditation upon the beauty of the opposite sex, which causes each one to wish above all things the embraces of the other and by common desire to carry out all of love's precepts in the other's embrace.[1]

Medieval ideas of beauty will be familiar to anyone who consumes social media or walks through a department store today. Blonde hair, fair skin, and a clear complexion were prized, as demonstrated in medieval art and literature, as well as books on cures and cosmetics. A beautiful woman was one who had smallish, perky breasts—often compared to apples—a small waist, and wide hips, while still looking dainty, of course. Ideally, her feet were small, but her belly was soft and round, unlike most cover models' today.

One lyricist, speaking to his "Helen," his "Venus," extols her many beautiful attributes, from her hair to her teeth:

Your golden locks hung marvelously,
your throat gleamed like a bank of snow,
your breast was slender. . . .
Stars radiated in your happy face;
Your teeth rivaled ivory in their hue.
The twinned beauty of your limbs exceeds my telling.
No wonder these qualities cast a spell on everyone.[2]

*This depiction of the legend of Hermaphroditus and Salmacis
demonstrates the beauty standards and ideal physiques of the day.*
L'Épître Othéa, fol. 132v, c. 1410–14 (detail)
British Library, London; Harley 4431

A less-enthusiastic poet says simply, "I fell in love with your hair / for it was blond."[3]

The handsomest medieval men were tall, slim, and broad-shouldered—attributes still valued in movie stars and models. Their physical strength was illustrated by their prowess and stamina on the battlefield, and while the perfect woman's belly was round, men in medieval art sometimes had six-pack abs—even Jesus himself. The famous knight and marshal of France Jean II Le Meingre, known as Boucicaut, was described by his biographer as very attractive:

> His physique is lean, but well built: he is athletic, and sturdy. He is broad in the chest, with wide and muscular shoulders; his hips, his thighs and his calves are sinewy.... His face is uniformly handsome, lightly tanned, with a becoming flush, having a good beard, auburn in colour.[4]

Predictably, medieval sources focus less often on men's appearances than on women's, as beauty was tied to a woman's inherent worth.

Science has shown that modern people who are born with features considered beautiful have an easier time in life, as they're perceived as both smarter and nicer, so perhaps we haven't advanced as far past the Middle Ages as we'd like to think. Fortunately, a person doesn't have to be born beautiful to achieve some of the benefits of the "halo effect." Good grooming can boost a person's perceived attractiveness, allowing them to reap a myriad of social benefits without plastic surgery.[5]

In the Middle Ages, people were already onto this idea, using a wide variety of personal grooming tools and methods to make themselves more attractive. Besides brushes, combs, and mirrors, archaeologists have found tweezers, and as we saw earlier, ear scoops.

Many examples of medieval tweezers have been found by archaeologists, illustrating medieval people's concern with removing both unsightly hairs and splinters.

Tweezers, 7th century
The Met Cloisters, New York

Well-groomed people were expected to comb both knots and nits out of their hair and beards, facilitated by the wide and fine teeth of combs like this one, meant for use by priests.

Double-sided ivory liturgical comb with scenes of Henry II and Thomas Becket, c. 1200–1210
The Met Cloisters, New York

The Book of the Civilised Man's advice for young men serving at table wouldn't seem out of place in a modern employee manual:

> Your hair should be neatly styled and evenly cut.
> A full beard should be trimmed if it becomes shaggy. . . .
> Your hands ought to be clean, and your sleeves should be laced.
> Do not let your nails be ugly or your teeth dirty.
> There should be no great number of long hairs in your nostrils. . . .
> Your tresses should not be blackened with soot. . . .
> There should not be any lice or dandruff in your beard or hair.[6]

While this baseline amount of personal grooming was acceptable, and insisted upon, there was a constant push-pull about altering a person's appearance for the sake of beauty or attractiveness. Priests condemned fashionable hairstyles and cosmetics, thundering from the pulpit about vanity and pride and spinning moral tales about women who, returning from the dead, re-lay the agonizing torments of demons who target their vain habits, stabbing them in the eyebrows with needles and tearing their hair.[7] Sir Geoffrey de la Tour Landry, a fourteenth-century French knight who wrote a treatise on good behavior for his daughters, tells a story about a woman who took so long to get ready for church that she held up the service. To teach her a lesson, the devil showed her his "hinder parts" in the mirror instead of her own face. "So foul and horrible were they," he continues, "that the lady went right out of her wits and stayed that way for a long time."[8] Such was the danger of aiming for perfection, like Lucifer himself.[9]

At the same time, the courtly love tradition encour-aged women to elevate their looks, both for the sake of beauty and for the power it would give them over men. Surviving recipes tell us about shampoos to enhance any hair color, masks and washes to erase freckles and wrin-kles, and techniques and pastes to whiten teeth.[10]

Beauty is only skin-deep, of course, and to care too much about our outward appearances runs the risk of de-valuing our inner selves. Obsessing over our perceived flaws can be extremely harmful to our mental health, as many of us have learned the hard way. Instead of worry-ing about unrealistic beauty standards, we should think of looking our best as presenting ourselves to the world in the way feel most comfortable—cosmetics or no cos-metics, hair or no hair, filter or no filter.

Dress to Impress

Medieval people were always cognizant of the social status that accompanied wealth, and never more so than while trolling for marriage prospects who might bring additional money and prestige to themselves and their families. For this reason, fine fabrics like silk and velvet embellished with precious metals, jewels, and furs were always in fashion, with changing styles allowing for different ways to show off how many yards of expensive textiles a person could afford. These ranged from creative slashing that revealed a second layer of sumptuous cloth to trailing sleeves and trains to the iconic long-toed shoes of the fourteenth century. Elab-

The textures of medieval clothing spoke to the wealth of the wearer, as in this portrait.
Workshop of Rogier van der Weyden (1399/1400–1464)
Portrait of Isabella of Portugal, c. 1450
Getty Museum, Los Angeles

Priests were unimpressed by both the elaborate hats and
scandalously short tunics of high society, which they
considered immoral.
Chroniques (Book Three), fol. 288v, c. 1480–83 (detail)
Getty Museum, Los Angeles; Ludwig XIII 7

orate hats likewise exuded wealth and style, and the increasingly expensive and extravagant headpieces of
medieval women served the dual purpose of being fashionable and counterbalancing their looks to give the
illusion of a narrower waist—a trick both modern fashion
designers and drag queens employ to fabulous advantage.

Like cosmetics, fashion was a constant source of ir-
ritation to those who took it upon themselves to police
people's morals. La Tour Landry shares an anecdote of a
young woman who lost her chance at a good marriage because she didn't dress appropriately for the cold and her
suitor thought she looked too pale. "It's a great folly," he
admonishes, "to wear thin clothes to make your body look

Prowess and Boldness, here personified, demonstrate the tight leggings and short tunics of medieval couture, proving that style and fierceness were not mutually exclusive.

Le Chemin de Vaillance, fol. 103v, before 1483 (detail)
British Library, London; Royal 14 E II

better."[11] Women were criticized for wearing clothes that were too fashionable, as well as for not wearing their best clothes to church.[12] One chronicler, John of Reading, declared that the Black Death was brought on by fashionable men "who wore their hose so tight they could not kneel down to pray."[13] If you're going to be fashionable, says La Tour Landry, at least wait until a trend catches on:

> The sin lies with those who first wear such clothing. Good and wise women should fear wearing such fashions until everyone wears them commonly because according to the word of God, the first will be the most blamed but the last will sit on the high seat.[14]

One respectable gift a lover might bestow was a mirror, like this one, with the backing carved in ivory.
Mirror cover with hawking scene, c. 1325–50
Walters Art Museum, Baltimore

Being ahead of the trend might be a sin, but being on trend was respectable.

As medieval people scanned each other for signs of fashion-forwardness, wealth, and status, they were also searching for signs of attachment, much like people today will look for a wedding ring on the hand of someone they're interested in. While a married person in the Middle Ages might indeed wear a wedding ring, this was not a universal practice at the time. Instead, their attachment might be evident in the form of a love token.

According to Marie, Countess of Champagne, who presides over imagined trials in *The Art of Courtly Love*, there is a wide range of acceptable love tokens, many of which could be worn on the body:

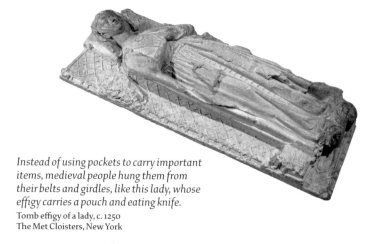

Instead of using pockets to carry important items, medieval people hung them from their belts and girdles, like this lady, whose effigy carries a pouch and eating knife.
Tomb effigy of a lady, c. 1250
The Met Cloisters, New York

A woman who loves may freely accept from her lover the following: a handkerchief, a fillet for the hair, a wreath of gold or silver, a breastpin, a mirror, a girdle, a purse, a tassel, a comb, sleeves, gloves, a ring, a compact, a picture, a wash basin, little dishes, trays, a flag as a souvenir, and . . . any little gift which may be useful for the care of the person or pleasing to look at or which may call the lover to her mind.[15]

As Marie suggests, one of the more ambiguous love tokens was something that women wore every day: a girdle.[16] Pretty much every woman in the Middle Ages wore a girdle—or belt—as a way of both cinching garments at the waist and carrying objects like keys, purses, needles, or even books in a time before pockets were ubiquitous. (Women's garments still tend to suffer from a distinct lack of pockets.) Expensive, elaborate, or sentimental girdles were also given as engagement or wedding gifts from grooms to brides, so a fancy girdle on a woman could be a symbol that she was "taken," as it were. On the other hand, because these girdles could be so fancy and expensive, they were often passed down to daughters or other family members in wills, so a woman with a finely made girdle might only be wearing her best outfit. Medieval singles were better off hunting for more clues before jumping to conclusions.

Sometimes given as bridal gifts, girdles could be both expensive and sentimental objects, later bequeathed to a lady's cherished relatives or friends.
Fragment of a girdle, c. 1500
The Met Cloisters, New York

For women, the clearest sign that a man's affections were tied up was if he wore a favor. This wasn't just the stuff of literature and romance—knights really were meant to show devotion by wearing a token of their lady's love into tournament or battle. A favor could be an item from a lady's wardrobe, such as a handkerchief or detachable sleeve embroidered with her colors, that waved like a banner from her paramour's helmet. It could also be something worn closer to the body, like a ring or pin.[17]

The way we adorn ourselves today is still meant to send out signals to those we encounter on a daily basis. Conventional wisdom dictates that we should dress for the job we want, or even the partner we want, but freedom of expression means we can also dress for the identity we want—something denied to most medieval people whose wardrobes were in large part dictated by their station in life.

While medieval nobles were likely more consistent in their everyday attire—they were always on the job, in a

Ladies gave knights favors to wear into tournament or battle, such as a sleeve or scarf that could trail dramatically like banners.
Arthurian Romances, fol. 178r, c. 1290–1300 (detail)
Yale University Library, New Haven, CT; Beineke 229

sense—we have the freedom, flexibility, and sheer wardrobe size to create looks to suit any occasion, relationship, or expression of identity.

When it comes to successful wooing in the modern world, the best fashion advice is to wear whatever makes you feel good. We look our best when we feel our best, and we feel our best when we're expressing our true selves.

Express Yourself

In addition to our clothing choices, we humans are constantly sending out physical signals that reveal our thoughts, feelings, and intentions, and these are never more potent than when we are trying to attract a lover.

To impress someone with body language in the Middle Ages was to exhibit a high degree of self-control. Body movements were meant to be slow and measured, with no excessive frivolity. "As you are speaking," says Daniel of Beccles, "still your hands and feet."[18]

In his advice to his daughters, La Tour Landry also emphasizes stillness as an attractive quality, especially when it comes to a person's gaze:

> Daughters, don't be like the tortoise or the crane, which turn their heads here and there like a weathervane. . . . Always look directly in front of you and if you must look to the side, turn your face and your body together, holding yourself firm and sure, for those who frivolously cast their eyes about and turn their faces here and there are mocked.[19]

La Tour Landry drives this point home by telling the apocryphal story of the king of Denmark's three daughters who were put forth as potential matches for the king of England. One of the daughters was eliminated from the field because she moved her head and eyes too much, demonstrating that she wasn't steadfast enough to be queen material. (The second princess talked too much, of course.)

Excessive laughter was also a sign of ill-refinement, which is perhaps why no one mentioned they were looking for a marriage partner with a great sense of humor. The well-mannered, says Daniel of Beccles, should laugh only in a controlled and intelligent way:

> When you laugh, let the sound out delicately.
> A level-headed man should laugh modestly,
> as the brainless usually shake with boisterous
> guffaws.[20]

Although a person's laughter should be "sincere," mouths should stay closed so as to not show teeth.[21] Heaven forbid that a person should let loose with their merriment.

When it came to romance, part of the reason people were measured in their body language was because true love—that is, adulterous courtly love—was meant to be kept secret. "When made public," Andreas Capellanus asserts, "love rarely endures."[22]

Nevertheless, there are some tells that are hard to hide. Lovers, we are told, turn pale, don't eat or sleep well, have heart palpitations, become ill, and age quickly. They may also spend more time on personal grooming than before.[23] Ladies may play with their hair, bite their lips, and steal glances, while men may experience a decline in their martial prowess—at least while they're pining.[24]

If you're into someone, it's best to ignore Andreas's advice and let the person know. Body language is one of the easiest ways to send a signal, and some of the medie-

Although adultery was idealized in tales of courtly love,
as here in the story of Tristan and Isolde, in reality it was
considered sinful and was punishable by the church.
Jeanne de Montbaston (active 1320–55), *Roman du Bon Chevalier
Tristan, Fils au Bon Roy Meliadus de Leonois*, fol. 85r, c. 1320–40 (detail)
Getty Museum, Los Angeles; Ludwig XV 5

val observations on expressing attraction might actually
do the trick: playing with your hair, stealing glances, and
touching your own face are all places to start a flirtation
with someone.[25] Once you've established that sparks may
be flying, it's time to get brave and take the next step.

Use Your Words

Modern dating apps often give prompts to get the conversational ball rolling, including things like "How do you like to spend the weekend?" and "What did your favorite teacher say about you?" For medieval people, the safest place to find common ground was interests and hobbies. Hawking and hunting were both good getting-to-know-you activities as well as conversational subjects, while topics like religion and politics were potential hot buttons, especially depending on the political and religious climate of the day. Gossip was technically sinful, but talking about friends and acquaintances has always been an easy conversational in.

Unlike in the modern world of dating, as we briefly saw, in medieval love treatises a sense of humor was not considered a desirable attribute; however, a clever turn of phrase has been a successful way to flaunt intelligence for millennia. "Always season your refined speech with wit," advises Daniel of Beccles, but at the same time, "Withhold a sense of frivolity from each topic."[26] He tells his schoolboys:

> Anything you say should be entertaining, polite, and sophisticated.
> No filthy speech should come out of your mouth.
> Foul language clashes unharmoniously with a distinguished tongue.
> Obscene speech fouls the speaker more often than the listener. . . .
> No one should hear libellous songs, blasphemy, or scandals from you.[27]

Foul and *obscene* may refer to sex or the body, as we tend to use these words now, but they may also mean swearing or blasphemy. In the Middle Ages, most swearing actually was blasphemy. Legendary English knight

William Marshal's biography, for example, is peppered with knights and kings exclaiming things like "God's teeth!" to show surprise or displeasure.[28] Using God's name in vain meant breaking one of the Ten Commandments, so naturally, such swearing was considered uncouth, like dropping four-letter words today in front of grandmothers or at the office. On the other hand, bodily and sexual humor that we might find more taboo, especially at work, was an essential part of medieval culture, although euphemisms were preferred in polite society, as we shall see.

For women it was not necessarily what they talked about, but how much—or rather, how little—they spoke that made them marriage material. Women were believed to be excessively chatty by nature, so they were constantly admonished to curb and censor their speech. La Tour Landry says to his daughters, "Don't be too full of words, for one who speaks too much isn't thought to be wise."[29] He is a stickler on this point and relates that in his younger days, he rejected a woman as a marriage partner because she was both too chatty and too forward: "She was full of words. When we had to leave, she was pert,

Meeting a potential partner could be a conversational gauntlet in which a lady had to ensure she spoke just enough and on the correct topics.
Cent Balades d'Amant et de Dame, fol. 376r, c. 1410–14 (detail)
British Library, London; Harley 4431

asking me two or three times not to leave but to come see her." For La Tour Landry, this was unbearably aggressive and spoke ill of her character overall. He concludes that he dodged a bullet in rejecting this woman, because soon afterward she became the center of a scandal and then she died, presumably getting her just deserts in the afterlife.[30]

What La Tour Landry is trying to drive home is the importance of using your words correctly to net yourself a decent spouse. But keeping passionate declarations to a minimum was critical during medieval courtship for a more important reason: preventing accidental marriage.

For a marriage to be valid, medieval law only required two freely consenting adults expressing their desire to marry, then following it up with sexual intercourse.[31] Even if the words were conditional or referred to some future date, to voice any intent to marry and then have sex was to actually *be* legally married. While many weddings took place on the porch of the church and were presided over by a priest and witnessed by guests, none of these things was strictly necessary. The ease with which people could be married created a confusing legal nightmare that could easily be exploited, as Elizabeth Woodville's detractors did during the Wars of the Roses when they called her

Arthurian romances served as inspiration for both men and women who wished to emulate their chivalric roles. This casket shows scenes from the story of Lancelot.
Casket, c. 1330–50
Walters Art Museum, Baltimore

secret marriage to Edward IV into question. That Edward had expressed intent to marry another woman before Elizabeth cast further doubt on the legality of their union, leaving the door open for Richard III to call their children bastards and usurp the throne upon Edward's death.[32]

In the same century, Margery Paston, a member of an up-and-coming Norfolk family, secretly married a family servant named Richard Calle, bringing shame on her more class-conscious relatives. Her mother appealed to the local bishop to annul the marriage based on the hope that it had been conducted improperly. Determined, Margery, "rehearsed what she had said [to the bishop and] if those words made it not sure, she said boldly . . . that she would make it surer before she went thence." The bishop found that no repetition was necessary: Margery and Richard had said they wanted to be married, then they consummated the marriage. There was nothing the family could do to separate the happy couple.[33]

Luckily for us, lusty words between consenting adults behind a haystack are no longer legally binding, but medieval headaches around marriage have left a lasting impression. Some weddings are still preceded by the reading of the banns for three weeks, and wedding guests are often invited to voice their objections before a couple's vows are exchanged—remnants of a time when people could be married by accident.

While the spoken word was, clearly, an extremely important part of medieval love affairs, the best place for us to get in touch with medieval ideas—and ideals—around love from this distance is through the written word. It's no coincidence that the term *romance*, which once meant a story written in vernacular language (i.e., not in Latin), now solely refers to love stories. Tales of Lancelot and Guinevere, Tristan and Isolde, and Robin and Marian continue to be told and retold with each new generation.

Love letters were very much a part of medieval romance,
in both literature and the real world. Here a lady named
Lucretia receives a letter from her lover via a messenger and
her maid and, regretting a fit of pique in which she's torn it
up, places it carefully in a chest.
Historia de Duobus Amantibus, fol. 30r, c. 1460–70
Getty Museum, Los Angeles; MS 68

Lancelot himself was created in the simmering cauldron of the courtly love aesthetic in twelfth-century France, emerging alongside the vibrant lyrics of the troubadours, who valorized the potency and tragedy of adulterous love. Unlike a wandering minstrel, a troubadour had a place at court writing and performing entertaining songs, and while his subjects could vary widely, the most popular were, of course, about love. Troubadours are credited with shaping the ideals of courtly love and reinforcing the rules for loving correctly, including that it should cause suffering and be adulterous.[34] One of the most famous troubadours, Marcabru, writes,

> I'll tell you how love consumes us.
> It sings to you; it ogles the other;
> It talks with you; it flirts with another. . . .
> It will lie straighter than a line
> Before you become its friend.[35]

As this verse illustrates, courtly love is consuming, flirty, and suggestive, without overtly spelling things out. Euphemisms like the one used here were a handy means of communication in a courtly love context, as they required playfulness and wit and allowed for some plausible deniability in case a lady—or her husband—took offense.

While the goal of courtly love was ostensibly a successful seduction, the focus of troubadour poetry is mostly on the suffering of love and the anticipation—or fantasy—of being with the beloved, much like today's hit love songs. Like an earnest modern suitor with a playlist (or a guitar and a TikTok account), medieval lovers could sing these flirty songs to the object of their affection, making their feelings known, and, not coincidentally, elevating the fame of the artist.

In a time before telephones and cars, letters—like songs—were another important part of courtship, especially as circumstances could frequently see lovers far from home.[36] Medieval love letters, even between affectionate spouses, may seem a little dry to our eyes due to some cultural conventions, and because many were dictated to or read out by a scribe, not handwritten by the sender. Other medieval love letters are everything a troubadour could hope for, like this one:

> Why do you make delay so long, so far away? Why do you want your only one to die, who as you know, loves

you with soul and body, who sighs for you at every hour, at every moment, like a hungry little bird.[37]

As many modern texters have learned the hard way, writing your most heartfelt and raciest feelings down leaves them open to being seen by eyes other than those intended, so it's wise to calculate the risks before committing anything to words. After all, unlike troubadour songs that are mainly fantasy, letters focus on a real desire for their authors to see and enjoy each other. The letter above is a case in point, sent as it was from one medieval nun to another at the risk of censure and possible punishment for what would have been considered a sinful love at the time. But, as writers have been saying for millennia, love tends to overrule our better judgment, a truth we can see for ourselves every day. In the words of troubadour Bernart de Ventadorn, "whoever loves has lost his mind."[38]

Whatever your love language, whether it's lyrics, letters, or a quick and flirty text, using caring words to express your affection is one of the best ways to ensure your beloved understands your feelings and is on the same page. When it comes to words in any time period, there is nothing more romantic than an enthusiastic yes.

Of all the advice in this book, the guidelines of courtly love might be the least beneficial to apply to modern life, as some deeply entrenched medieval ideas around love—that it involves suffering and secrecy and is overwhelming to the point that people are not responsible for their actions—are ones that we are actively working to overcome as a society. Still, there are things we can take from our long human history of romance that are always true: It's easiest to attract a lover if you're looking and feeling your best, it's good to send flirty signals to let them know you're into them, and it's best to make sure you're communicating your feelings and your needs to your partner in words.

HOW TO FIGHT

Since nobility of courage has chosen the knight over those who are beneath him in servitude, nobility of habits and good manners befit the knight, for nobility of courage could not achieve the high honour of Chivalry without appropriate virtue and good habits.
        —Ramon Llull, *The Book of the Order of Chivalry*

hivalry today denotes romance, politeness, and good manners, but this is only one side of the medieval coin. The word *chivalry* comes from the French *cheval*, meaning "horse": there is no chivalry without knights—that is, mounted warriors. The modern adage about being "a lover, not a fighter" suggests there is a dichotomy, but in the Middle Ages, the ideal knight needed to be a lover *and* a fighter. Training to be good at both started very early.

Serve, Then Protect

L ike all medieval children, noble boys started life in a female orbit, whether they were raised by their mothers, a wet nurse, a nursemaid, or a combination of all three. Around the age of seven, noble children were often fostered by other families in order to learn different techniques and skills and to build relationships through sharing bed and board. Sometimes, high-status nobles fostered several children at once, creating more opportunities for friendships that might later solidify into alliances and even advantageous marriages. Thirteenth-century author Ramon Llull writes, "The knight must entrust his son to another knight so that he can learn how to carve at table and maintain a horse, and everything else that pertains to the honour of the knight."[1] This was a normal part of medieval culture among the aristocracy, and wasn't a sign of dislike or disinterest on the part of parents; rather, it was the chance to give their children the best possible opportunities for renown, stability, and prosperity. When William Marshal left home to be fostered, his biographer writes, "William couldn't wait to go, but when it came to the leave-taking his mother and sisters and all his brothers wept piteously—as is natural."[2]

The central skill of knighthood was horsemanship, as we've seen, and this is where training began. "A knight who has no horse is not suited to the office of Chivalry," declares Llull, and "if a child does not learn to ride in his youth [. . .] he shall not be able to learn when he is older."[3] In battle, a knight was utterly dependent on his horse, which was more than just a mode of transportation. When asked once why he was putting on his armor after he mounted his horse, Geoffrey, Duke of Brittany, replied, "It's all very well being armed when you're in danger, but if your horse is too far away when your enemy attack, they'll capture you in no time—you'll be in much less trouble if you're mounted."[4]

Destriers or warhorses were expensive commodities, having been specifically bred for purpose and trained for at least five years.[5] Not only did a destrier need to learn to carry the weight of a fully armed knight, with saddle, padding, and its own armor, while maneuvering in tight spaces, but it also needed to keep calm and steady in the crush and noise of war without bolting, rearing, or unseating its rider. One of William Marshal's horses reputedly managed to stand its ground during an attack by four knights: "Despite their blows the horse wouldn't budge an inch: he'd respond only to the Marshal's spurs."[6] The finest destriers, in addition to being fiercely obedient, were also trained to execute their own offensive maneuvers, including stomping, jumping, and kicking, both forward and backward. Some of the most impres-

Said to have been "the greatest knight,"
William Marshal epitomized the ideals of
chivalry in his own generation, as well as
those following.
Effigy in the round (before bomb damage), c. 1219
Temple Church, London

sive feats of show horses today are the techniques that were once used in medieval warfare, now performed to delight audiences at medieval and horse-themed events.

Like his destrier, a young knight-to-be learned to carry the weight of armor and weapons, with both made to fit his growing body. It's a modern myth that medieval armor was difficult to fight in: chain mail bent and flowed easily around the body, while plate was fastened with buckles and straps to make it easy to maneuver in. A well-outfitted knight would use a combination of both mail and plate: the mail to stop slashes, cuts, and stabs; the plate to deflect blows and prevent broken bones. The quilted gambeson he wore under the plate, which kept the metal from digging into his skin, added to the weight; however, modern reconstructions suggest that a knight in full kit wasn't carrying more than about eighty pounds on his body, an amount that—while not negligible—is comparable to the weight carried by soldiers from the ancient world to the present day.

In addition to being the most important symbol of knighthood and the origin of the word chivalry, *horses were fierce fighters in their own right.*
Bestiary, fol. 42v, 1225–50 (detail)
British Library, London; Royal 12 F XIII

Heraldry could entail simple colors and shapes or symbols of a family's reputation or legend. This knight's heraldic fashion choices ensure that he will still be known if he loses his banner and shield.

Codex Manesse, fol. 160v, c. 1300–40 (detail)
Heidelberg University Library, Germany; Cod. Pal. German 848

One of the most popular texts in medieval Europe was a manual for warfare called *De Re Militari* by Publius Flavius Vegetius Renatus (known simply as Vegetius), which although it outlined ancient Roman and Greek techniques, served as a blueprint for medieval military strategy and thought. Vegetius says,

> Recruits and novice soldiers were trained morning and afternoon in all types of arms, but veterans and trained soldiers also exercised with their arms once a day without fail. For length of time or number of years does not transmit the art of war, but continual exercise. No matter how many years he has served, an unexercised soldier is forever a raw recruit.[7]

Although medieval knights were not soldiers in the Roman or modern sense,[8] they were likely to have taken Vegetius's advice to heart, training every day with the possible exception of holy days. After all, becoming fast and proficient in arms was a matter of survival. "Speed is

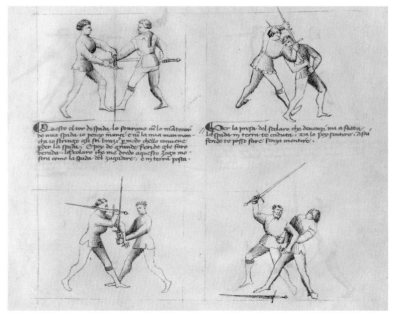

Knights spent many years perfecting their martial techniques.
Il Fior di Battaglia by Fiore Furlan dei Liberi da Premariacco,
shown here, is one of the earliest surviving books detailing the
techniques of sword combat.
Fior di Battaglia, fol. 30r, c. 1410 (detail)
Getty Museum, Los Angeles; Ludwig XV 13

acquired through bodily exercise itself," Vegetius writes,
"and also the skill to strike the enemy whilst covering
oneself, especially in close-quarters sword fighting."

As to how a knight should be trained, Vegetius gives us
more clues:

> It is advisable that they should very frequently be felling
> trees, carrying burdens, jumping ditches, swimming in
> the sea or rivers, marching at full step or even running
> in their arms, with their packs on. The habit of daily
> labour in peace may not then seem arduous in war.[9]

Elite warrior and marshal of France, Jean II le Meingre (known as "Boucicaut") was admired and respected by his peers. He is seen here praying to Saint Catherine.

Heures de Maréchal de Boucicaut, miniature, c. 1410–15 (detail)
Musée Jacquemart-André, Paris

That Vegetius's training advice was at least somewhat influential during the Middle Ages is evident in the biography of Boucicaut, the handsome French knight we met in chapter two. According to his biographer,

He would train himself to leap fully armed onto his horse's back, or on other occasions he would go for long runs on foot, to increase his strength and resistance, or he would train for hours with a battle-axe or a hammer to harden himself to armour and to exercise his arms and hands, so that he could easily raise his

Lady Courtesy extends a dance invitation to a lover who treats her with due respect.
Roman de la Rose, fol. 9v, c. 1405 (detail)
Getty Museum, Los Angeles; Ludwig XV 7

arms when fully armed. . . . He could do a somersault fully armed but for his [helmet], and he could dance equipped in a coat of mail.

Boucicaut was also said to have been able to shimmy up between two walls without assistance and to climb a ladder from the underside with just one hand—two if he was armed. Although this might seem like hyperbole, modern experiments with fourteenth-century armor have shown this was all very possible—even the dancing.[10]

Dancing might seem like a strange thing to do in armor, but it is a good reminder of the other side of the knightly coin: refinement befitting a noble. In addition to the lessons meted out on the training grounds, a noble boy would be expected to continue his education through books, while also learning to sing and dance. Dancing was considered a chivalrous activity because spending

time with fine ladies was thought to inspire men to love—
and to fight. One spontaneous dance party that preceded
a tournament gave the English enough spirit to soundly
trounce the competition, since "the ladies redoubled the
strength, the spirit, the courage and the heart of every
knight present."[11] In addition to making boys agile and
light on their feet, being able to dance well was a sign of
good breeding, and one of many skills knights were expected to have mastered before earning their spurs.

Boys destined for knighthood would also have an up
close and personal introduction to table manners in
their role as cupbearers. By attending their lords at table,
these boys would learn how best to hold their utensils,
serve their dining partners, make polite conversation,
and flirt. After dinner, they would also have the pleasure
of remaining in the hall while minstrels and storytell-
ers spun tales of the greatest knights: Gawain, Lancelot,
and Tristan. They would learn from these legends that
even the best of the best were subject to fall at the turn
of Fortune's wheel, and while flirtation is noble and fun,
disloyally crossing the line into outright adultery breaks
the vital bonds of society and can bring disaster, even at a
court as perfect as Camelot. Both entertaining and mor-
ally educational, these stories provided inspiration to
those at the highest tables, as well as those young boys
who stood back, rapt.

As boys grew into teens, both their service and education as fighters continued as they took on the role of
squires, responsible for the care of a knight's weapons,
equipment, and horses. Some men never advanced past
the rank of squire, remaining support staff instead of
ascending the social ladder, but for most, squiring was a
stepping stone on the path to becoming what they most
wanted to be: a true knight.

The knighthood ceremony, like most rituals in medi-

eval Europe, was intimately tied to the Christian faith.
Given that young men had trained half their lives for this
moment, it was a suitably serious and lengthy process.
Geoffroi de Charny, a famed warrior and the author of
a manual for fourteenth-century French knights called
The Book of Chivalry, gives us a detailed look into the ritual, beginning with the night before. That evening, the
squire would give confession, then bathe as a metaphor-
ical and literal cleansing before going to bed on "clean,
white sheets." In the morning, knights were to attend
him, dressing him in "new, white, and clean material,
signifying that they should all from henceforth keep
themselves pure and free from sin." Over these under-
garments, the squire was clothed in a red tunic and black
hose, representing the blood he was to shed and the
earth, always waiting to receive him in death. Finally,
he was dressed in a white belt, for chastity, and red mantle, for humility, at which point he would be escorted to
church for a vigil that was to last all night. In the morning, the squire would hear mass, and the actual ceremony would begin.

*Symbols of the horsemanship inherent to knighthood, spurs were
given to young men when they were knighted.*
Pair of rowel spurs, 15th century
The Met Cloisters, New York

A person could be knighted on the battlefield for acts of great bravery.
Here, Richard II knights his cousin, the future Henry V, on horseback.
La Prinse et mort du roy Richart (Book of the Capture and Death of King Richard II),
fol. 5r, c. 1401–5 (detail)
British Library, London; Harley 1319

Only knights could confer knighthood—kings being
knights themselves—which meant that it was knights
who fastened gold spurs to the squire's feet, to rid him
of any further monetary greed, and gave him a sword
to represent "right, reason, and justice." Then the one
conferring the knighthood kissed the squire "as a sign
of confirmation [of] . . . peace, love, and loyalty," and
either tapped him with a sword or slapped his face, so
that, as Ramon Llull explains, "He will remember what
he is promising and the great burden he must carry and
the great honour he is taking through the Order of Chivalry."[12] After this emotional moment, the culmination of
years of blood, sweat, and tears, Llull says it was time to

party: "That day a great festival shall be celebrated with gift-giving, banquets . . . and everything else that befits a chivalric festival."[13]

Since knighthoods were usually bestowed upon dozens of young men at once, it was a great opportunity for them to show off their impeccable table manners in front of their fellow knights, the king, and the ladies as they celebrated their great achievement. It's a good thing they'd already learned how to dance.

As the journey from boyhood to knighthood demonstrates, putting in our reps is essential if we want to accomplish anything, and becoming the best can take many years. For those of us who want to keep expanding our capabilities, the training never stops. No matter what we wish to achieve, it's important to learn from those around us, round out our expertise with complementary skills, and then show up each day with the drive to improve. Although milestones are important and it's worthwhile to celebrate them, it's devotion to practice that will give us both the skills and the resilience to succeed when we put ourselves to the test.

Win Renown

In order to fulfill their societal role, knights needed to be ready to fight at all times, which meant keeping both their weapons and their skills sharp. Despite what medieval romances would have us believe, knights didn't just wander around looking for an ogre to fight. Instead, during times when there was no outright warfare in the region and no active crusades, knights competed in tournaments in order to test themselves, show off their prowess, and—although it was ill-mannered to say it aloud—gain wealth.

These days, jousting is considered the centerpiece of the tournament and the unmissable main event of medieval fairs and shows. In this iconic medieval sport, two mounted knights charge each other at full gallop, using lances to unseat their opponent. Geoffroi de Charny calls the joust "the first exercise in the use of arms which [knights] can encounter . . . and they are eager to do it."[14] Proficiency at jousting was fundamental for medieval knights, as it was practice for the cavalry charge, the opening gambit of many a pitched battle. Given that lances could be up to eighteen feet long,[15] it was essen-

Jousting gave knights opportunities to show their prowess, impressing their peers and potential marriage partners at the same time.
Le Duc des Vrais Amants, fol. 150r, c. 1410–14 (detail)
British Library, London; Harley 4431

tial to practice with them as often as possible if a knight was going to wield one successfully in the chaos of real combat. Modern jousts resemble late medieval jousts of peace in which lances were blunted and a tilt barrier was put in place to keep knights and horses from crashing into each other with truly catastrophic results.

In the early days of the tournament, however, the focus was not on one-on-one jousting, but on the mêlée.

The mêlée was a mock battle in which groups of knights charged each other with lances in an open field. After the first pass, the knights continued to fight using swords and other weapons on horseback and on foot until they captured their opponents. Although the aim was not to kill the other team, the mêlée was still an extraordinarily brutal event. The biographer of William Marshal gives us a description of one tournament in bone-crushing detail:

The noise was deafening! All were bent on landing mighty blows; what a shattering of lances you'd have heard, the stumps and shards so littering the ground that the horses were stopped in their tracks. In the heaving throng that filled the plain the companies bawled their battle cries. . . . You'd have seen knights' bridles being seized, other knights being rescued, horses running in all directions, pouring sweat. . . . [I]t was a splendid tournament indeed.[16]

In a joust of peace, conducted for sport, lances were tipped with heads that would diffuse the blow, like this one.

Lance head for the tournament, c. 1475–1525
The Met Cloisters, New York

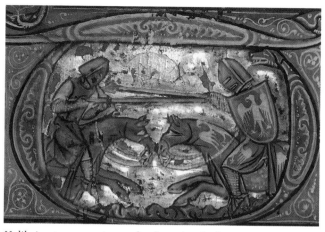

Unlike in a tournament, a cavalry charge involved sharp lances meant to pierce armor at high speed.
Vidal Mayor, fol. 229r, c. 1290–1310 (detail)
Getty Museum, Los Angeles; Ludwig XIV 6

Defeated knights were taken back to the victors' home base and not permitted to leave until they were ransomed. Usually, defeat meant forfeiting your destrier, a truly painful loss given the expense, training, and care put into a warhorse, not to mention any sentimental feelings a knight might have toward his own. It might also mean losing equipment and money. Unchivalrous knights, therefore, disregarded the honor system that was to hold them in captivity, escaping with their horses and money, but risking a serious impact on their reputation.

Mêlée combat was a good opportunity for knights to practice the skills they'd need in battle, like teamwork and holding formations. It was also a place where knights could put their mettle to the test, learn new skills, and discover the strengths and weaknesses of the other knights they might fight alongside or against in future warfare.

Beyond the combat itself, there was much to be learned from the business conducted in the aftermath:

> They all had work to do: a mighty throng, bigger than at a fair, swarmed about seeing friends taken prisoner in the fray, or hunting for lost equipment; many were asking on every side for news of friends or kinsmen and who their captors were, while the captured were seeking bail or ransom from friends or acquaintances.[17]

Settling accounts and ransoms after the battle was over gave knights the opportunity to practice negotiating, valuing, and navigating the minefield of personal relationships, all of which would serve them well as fighters or as lords.

Vegetius stresses that soldiers should be sent into intense battle "only after being blooded in smaller-scale conflicts,"[18] and the mêlée was intended to serve this purpose, preparing knights to fight through chaos and confusion, pain and blood, victory and defeat.

While most of us will thankfully never face such dangers, the principle of easing into difficult and unknown situations by stages is useful to bear in mind whenever we come up against challenges. "All arts," says Vegetius, "depend on practice."[19] Although most of our challenges will not actually be life-or-death, there is one thing that is universal to the human condition whether we're knights or ordinary people: fear.

Fight Your Fear

Courage was one of the essential qualities of medieval knights, and something they needed to draw upon again and again throughout their lives. One of the ways they managed this was through the gradual introduction to battle, as we've seen, through constant practice and the trial by fire of mêlée combat. But actual war was an entirely different thing. How did knights retain their courage under fire?

A fundamental pillar of strength for medieval knights was their faith—not only in God, but also in the justice of their cause. In late antiquity, Saint Augustine had outlined the requirements for a "just war," which included defending the innocent, fighting for the church, and fighting for your lord. A true knight had faith that if his king had called him up to fight, the cause would be just, and in any case, serving his king meant that he was fulfilling his duty. As Charny says,

As warriors, knights regularly had to fight fear, personified here as a fierce, armored woman with sword raised.

Roman de la Rose, fol. 136v, c. 1490–1500 (detail)
British Library, London; Harley 4425

This is the case when lords have wars, and their men can and should fight for them and move confidently and bravely into battle for such causes, for if one performs well there, one is honored in life, and if one dies there, one's soul is saved, if other sins do not stand in the way of this.[20]

If a knight lived his life well and did not dishonor himself by the manner in which he fought, that is, he could rely on the fact that he was on the side of the angels and would be provided for after death. This was a powerful spiritual comfort for men whose earthly fate was uncertain.

In addition to God and his king, a knight also placed his faith in his brothers-in-arms, from the leaders who sent him into danger to the men who fought at his side. Throughout his treatise on military strategy, Vegetius demonstrates the vital importance of morale in an army, saying, "It is a natural reaction in the minds of nearly all men to be fearful as they go to do battle with the enemy," but that fear itself could be fatal. To combat this, he advises leaders on a tactic that we have seen countless times in medieval movies: "An army gains courage and fighting spirit from advice and encouragement from their general, especially if they are given such an account of the coming battle as leads them to believe they will easily win a victory." Morale boosters within this speech should include "remind[ing] them of any occasion on which [the enemy has] been beaten by us in the past" and "provok[ing] hatred . . . by arousing their anger and indignation."[21]

Knightly inspiration could also be found by seeing someone within the company performing brave actions. This is a near-constant theme in the biography of William Marshal, whose author puts it bluntly: "The fact is, sirs, the prowess of a single valiant knight can embolden

Life as a knight meant risking injury and disability as well as death. The most admired and respected lords were those who cared for injured and elderly veterans.
Arthurian Romances, fol. 257v,
c. 1290–1300 (detail)
Yale University Library, New Haven, CT;
Beineke 229

a whole army."[22] Marshal often threw himself into the fray to inspire his comrades, just as another military leader—Joan of Arc—would do two centuries later.[23]

It wasn't just being inspired in the moment that allowed knights to gather their courage, but also the knowledge that they'd be cared for no matter the outcome. The reality of war meant that the knights who survived might experience physical and psychological injuries and need to be supported once they returned home. Legal contingencies were put into place to ensure a knight's assets would be tended to in the event of any incapacity, and some lords, like Boucicaut, took their support a step further:

> The marshal is particularly magnanimous towards veteran men-at-arms who were once valuable but are now infirm, and who, having failed to save money, are now poverty-stricken. . . . He does them honour, and helps them with pensions, and sees them looked after in their old age.

That assistance in the event of poverty or disability was an important concern of knights as they went to war is further emphasized by Boucicaut's biographer, who continues, "Seeing their leader exercise care of this sort, they will give him their love and affection[;] they will serve him with greater willingness."[24]

Finally, a knight who was to fight with courage and win needed to have an unshakable faith in himself and his abilities. Inner strength could sometimes come from using fear as fuel, "as trapped men draw extra courage from desperation, and when there is no hope, fear takes up arms."[25] It's much better, however, to feel confident before your back is up against the wall. Charny writes,

> When moving against your enemies to meet them in battle, never admit the idea that you might be defeated nor think how you might be captured or how you might flee, but be strong in heart, firm, and confident, always expecting victory, not defeat, whether or not you are on top, for whatever the situation, you will always do well because of the good hopes that you have.[26]

Although he realized that a positive mindset would not always be enough to win the day—which is why he also encourages placing your life in God's hands—Charny, like other chivalric writers, believed that it truly ain't over till it's over.

Those in the modern world who have experienced life-or-death situations can attest that courage means confronting the inevitability of fear and refusing to give up. Whether we find ourselves in a major crisis or a minor one, we can learn from those who have suffered the worst and survived: make contingency plans, take strength and inspiration from those around you, trust in yourself and your own abilities, and, as Geoffroi tells us, "always and in all circumstances be determined to do your best."[27]

Show Mercy

ven though modern media would have us believe that the job of medieval knights was chopping off limbs haphazardly and scowling, one of the most prized tenets of chivalry wasn't picking fights: it was showing mercy.

The noble boys who served at feasts would have heard many stories like the one from Thomas Malory's *Morte d'Arthur* in which a hotheaded Gawain takes revenge on a knight named Sir Blamoure, who has killed his hunting hounds. Blamoure yields and begs for mercy, but Gawain refuses to listen and swings his sword, intending to kill the knight. Instead, he accidentally beheads Blamoure's lady, who has thrown herself over her husband at the last minute. Stunned and ashamed, Gawain learns the price of reckless anger, as he is forced to ride to Camelot with the lady's head suspended round his neck. To drive home the lesson, Guinevere's ladies make him promise to always defend women and to never refuse mercy to any-

Members of the Order of the Garter, seen here in their insignia, were sworn to uphold the ideals of knighthood and revere Saint George, patron saint of England.

Statutes of the Order of the Garter, fol. 439r, 1444–45 (detail)
British Library, London; Royal 15 E VI

one who asks for it.[28] Gawain's story is a reminder to all of a knight's first duty: protecting the vulnerable.

While Gawain is a fictional character, it's clear that the knights of the Round Table served as both commentary on society as well as aspirational goals for the aristocracy. In the fourteenth century, the Order of the Garter was created by Edward III of England to celebrate knighthood and inspire good deeds after the manner of King Arthur's knights. Not to be outdone, Jean II of France created the Company of the Star shortly afterward, inspiring Geoffroi de Charny to write his guide for its members: *The Book of Chivalry*.[29] Both of these kings had fought in the bloody battles of the Hundred Years' War, so they were familiar with the horrors of warfare, but in their minds knighthood still retained the ideals evoked in story and song: honor, valor, justice, and mercy.

Although there was no universal "code of chivalry," the many treatises on knighthood, as well as the literature that reflects them, extol virtues beyond fighting skill. A knight's fundamental duty, whether in warfare or in his everyday life, was to defend those who did not have the abilities or the means to do so themselves.

"The most excellent and most noble order of knighthood was established," says Jean de Bueil, a respected fourteenth-century French commander, "in order to protect, safeguard, and defend the common people who are always the most damaged by the perils of war."[30] As most able-bodied men would have been called up to fight in a king's army no matter what their station in life, the common people Bueil refers to tended to be the impoverished, disabled, elderly, churchmen, women, and children. Ramon Llull says,

> It is the office of the knight to support widows, orphans and the helpless, for just as it is customary and right that the mighty help to defend the weak, and the

weak take refuge with the mighty, so it is customary in the Order of Chivalry that because it is great, honourable and powerful, it comes to the succour and aid of those who are inferior to it in honour and strength.[31]

Charny adds, "Above all refrain from enriching yourself at others' expense, especially from the limited resources of the poor."[32] In practice, knights were not above plundering the towns and villages, and even churches, they had conquered in war, but the best knights like William Marshal and Boucicaut were said to be above such base behavior.

When it came to ladies, chivalry, then as now, was a double-edged sword. Knights were meant to defend them from all difficulty, and in medieval society, sometimes this could be very useful. Boucicaut, hearing that ladies in Paris were being unjustly disinherited by immoral and powerful men, created an order of thirteen

While chivalry included good manners and mercy, it did not exclude military tactics such as pursuing a fleeing enemy.
Jeanne de Montbaston (active 1320–55), *Roman du Bon Chevalier Tristan*, fol. 139v, c. 1320–40 (detail) Getty Museum, Los Angeles; Ludwig XV 5

Knights were indeed meant to come to the aid of damsels in distress, as Saint George so ably does here.

Book of hours, fol. 18v, c. 1450–55
Getty Museum, Los Angeles; MS 2

knights whose mandate was to be the champion of any lady who needed one.[33] Because women were not trained to fight at the time—in the courts or on the field—having knights available to take up their causes must have been a relief to these Parisiennes.

On the other hand, knights were meant to take matters out of ladies' hands because they were seen as too physically and, crucially, *intellectually* weak to handle things themselves. "Since man possesses more common sense and understanding and is of a naturally stronger disposition than a woman," explains Llull, "this enables him to be better than a woman."[34]

Placing ladies on pedestals to be worshipped and served was not wholly complimentary, much as it might seem that way, since it implies that they are more beauty than brains, something very much in line with medieval beliefs about women. Medieval chivalry and courtly love also set up an explicit expectation that a lady owes love—not to mention sex—in return for loyalty or good service, turning kind deeds from gifts into invoices.[35] Knights such as Ulrich von Liechtenstein (unlike the charming character played by Heath Ledger in *A Knight's Tale*) refused to leave the women of their obsessions alone, believing that enough service and persistence would unlock a lady's affections, as if love and sex were prizes to be won.

Because modern ideas of chivalry have their roots in medieval culture, even modern people with deep beliefs in equality must be on the lookout for the ways in which traditional chivalry retains troubling echoes of a time when women were still considered property. Wooing a modern woman well means valuing her mind, not just her shape, and it definitely means respecting her wishes—and her autonomy.

Although real knights, being human, fell short of their ideals sometimes, having those ideals in the first place elevated knighthood from a group of men trained for combat to a class of men worth writing stories and songs about for the better part of a millennium.

Whatever our own careers, vocations, or relationships, what we can learn from medieval knighthood is that the way we perform our deeds elevates them beyond the actions themselves. Bringing our principles and values to bear is what makes our interactions more than just exchanges of information, goods, or sentiments until they become an expression of who we want to be in the world. Keeping these values front and center will fuel us through all those reps to put in to become proficient, give us the resiliency to test ourselves, and grant us courage to face our fears, big or small.

Knights could be called upon to defend the honor of others in need, as Sir Tristan does here.

Jeanne de Montbaston (active 1320–55), *Roman du Bon Chevalier Tristan, Fils au Bon Roy Meliadus de Leonois*, fol. 68r, c. 1320–40 (detail)
Getty Museum, Los Angeles; Ludwig XV 5

HOW TO RUN A HOUSEHOLD

The wise housewife must know everything about her household . . . so that she can direct and command her servants and so that her husband can always be reassured when he invites people for dinner.
   —Christine de Pizan, *The Book of the Three Virtues*

f you were to time-travel to the Middle Ages, it would certainly be more comfortable to find yourself joining the ranks of the landowning class rather than the peasantry. Landed wealth meant better food, better clothing, and much less physical labor, qualities of life that many of us dream about when we think about being rich. The most successful aristocrats had a clear understanding of their responsibilities to those who lived and worked on their land,

and took them seriously. At a time when a man's home was literally his castle, there was plenty for the nobility to do, as well as lots of advice on the right way to do it.

Raise (All) Your Children Right

According to the teachings of the medieval church, men were the rulers of their households, with authority over their wives, children, and everyone else. From castles to cottages, however, the everyday running of the household was left to women, who tended to children, servants, and supplies and ensured everything in the domestic sphere ran smoothly in order to free their husbands to oversee the running of the estate.

Both men and women were responsible for giving their children the advice and teaching needed to help them succeed in life.
Vidal Mayor, fol. 205r, c. 1290–1310 (detail)
Getty Museum, Los Angeles; Ludwig XIV 6

Arguably, the foremost duty of a lady of the house—or chatelaine, from the French *château,* meaning castle—was to bear heirs, which meant ensuring her dietary and physical regimens would allow her to become pregnant and carry a child to term. According to *The Trotula,* a collection of advice specializing in women's medicine, it was important for women to maintain a moderate weight and not exert themselves, although infertility might still occur naturally though complications like having a "slippery" womb. There is a modern misconception that the blame for infertility was always laid at women's feet; however, this thirteenth-century text states matter-of-factly that sometimes trouble conceiving could stem from the man's medical issues, not the woman's.

One of *The Trotula*'s remedies to aid conception involves "damp wool dipped in ass's milk" tied on the woman's navel "until she has intercourse," while another encompasses drinking wine mixed with the powdered "testicles of an uncastrated male pig or a wild boar" immediately after her period ends.[1] Let it not be said that the women of medieval Europe weren't committed.

Because the most valuable heirs were male, it was important for ladies to do their best to become pregnant with boys. *The Distaff Gospels,* a treasure trove of medieval superstitions,[2] says a woman should have sex in the morning to conceive a boy, the evening or night for a girl. She should also "clench her fists" during intercourse to ensure she would have a son, consolidating and conferring chivalric ideas of strength and military prowess upon him before he was even one complete cell.[3]

A pregnant woman's care included baths, foot rubs, and "light and readily digestible foods,"[4] as well as being shielded from unpleasant sights to avoid afflicting the baby with physical deformities or provoking miscarriage.

The announcement of a medieval pregnancy also

meant the beginning of the time-honored tradition of trying to determine the fetus's sex. The women of *The Distaff Gospels* say:

> You should sprinkle salt on [the pregnant woman's] head while she is sleeping, so gently that she is unaware of it. When she wakes, note what name she says first. If she says a man's name it will be a boy and if she says a woman's name it will be a girl.[5]

The Trotula, in a much more scientific-sounding passage, advises:

> Take water from a spring and let the woman extract two or three drops of blood or milk from her right side and let these be dropped in the water. And if they fall to the bottom, she is carrying a male; if they float on top, a female.[6]

Superstitions meant to reveal a baby's sex continue to be passed down at modern baby showers, and it's likely that medieval thinking around such rituals was similar to ours; that is, there are some people who are absolutely convinced that their favorite technique is unassailable, while others find such activities to be just harmless fun. Without ultrasound technology, no one could ever have been sure of the sex of an infant until it was born, but then again, it also meant that no one was subjected to the increasingly outlandish gender reveal stunts of the modern world, either.

Pregnant and laboring mothers were supported by the women of the community, including midwives, relatives, and of course, female servants—as well as sometimes being physically supported by a birth girdle. Holy objects kept in the care of the church, birth girdles were

*Children were cherished in the Middle Ages and given
opportunities to play and learn before they took on adult
responsibilities.*
Desiderio da Settignano (c. 1429–1464), *A Little Boy*, c. 1455–60
National Gallery of Art, Washington, DC

long strips of parchment covered in prayers, illustrations, and symbols meant to protect mother and baby
during what was always a risky endeavor. It was the
midwives who cut the umbilical cord, washed, swad-
dled, and even baptized the baby if it looked as though
it was at risk. By the Late Middle Ages, courtesy dictated
that babies be named after their godparents, something
that could become complicated, as in the case of one
noblewoman, whose sons ended up being named "Guy,
John, John, John, John, William, and William."[7]

Although infant mortality was very high in the Middle Ages, babies were loved and cared for, placed in cradles
and kept warm by the fire, sung to and rocked to sleep,
with wealthy parents even hiring a "rockster" for this purpose.[8] Parents held hopes and dreams for their children,
baptizing them early to make sure they reached heaven
and perhaps even indulging in little superstitions like
drying their son's "baptismal bonnet . . . on the tips of a
sharp and shiny sword [so he] will always be handsome

*Medieval children were supplied with toys considered
appropriate to their gender and station, like this little knight
who jousts with a wooden lance.*
Toy mounted knight, c. 13th–14th century
Walters Art Museum, Baltimore

and bold, and welcome amongst the nobility." Some parents left food near their children's cradles to appease any supernatural beings who might wish to steal, exchange, or harm them while they slept.[9]

The higher up the ranks of society, the more likely it was that day-to-day infant care was performed by a wet nurse or a nursemaid, allowing noble mothers to circumvent the natural birth control of breastfeeding so that they could soon be pregnant again—but even absent mothers were invested in providing the best for their babies, vetting wet nurses with care.[10] Children often shared nurses and were raised together, giving them a group of peers with whom to play and socialize that might include siblings, relatives, or other children of the household.

Modern research has shown how important it is to give children a good head start, which includes providing them with toys to support their development, something medieval parents and caregivers ensured. Toddlers were supplied with rattles and strings of amber or red coral beads to help with teething.[11] Girls were given dolls and miniature pots and pans, while boys were given toy knights and toy horses, helping them absorb the roles and values of chivalry from infancy. Other toys included tops, balls, and dice, and one later source even describes a pinwheel.[12] Children learned to play a host of games, such as nine men's morris, backgammon, checkers, and chess, and it was considered good for them to also spend time in free play outside. While the most precious heirs might have done this under close supervision, most boys and girls would have found some freedom outside to run, play ball, catch frogs, and climb trees.

Children were not considered miniature adults with the same capacity to reason, work, or focus, as previous generations of historians have speculated. Instead, they were encouraged to learn through play. "Great youth, that sweet enemy of good sense," says Christine de Pizan, "will often not allow children of even great intelligence to devote themselves to study because of the desire to play." She continues, "unless the fear of beatings keeps them there," reminding us that medieval parents and other caregivers, like teachers, very much approved of the proverb "spare the rod, spoil the child."[13] At the same time, many teachers were not in favor of a heavy-handed approach to discipline. Daniel of Beccles says:

Gentle correction is permissible for any teacher.
Students should first receive a lenient warning, not a painful punishment.
Most of the time, violent beatings keep students from learning.
All teachers should advise and teach their students

> with gentle, unwavering words and full lessons.
> This is the way to receive your due thanks and praise.[14]

Although children weren't expected to perform the same amount or type of work as their elders, raising them properly meant teaching them how to become responsible members of the household. Every child was given small tasks that suited their abilities and station, whether that was fetching and carrying, feeding animals, or caring for younger siblings. Girls of every social class learned early how to make textiles, starting at first with carding wool and graduating to spinning and eventually weaving. Even those activities that children might have undertaken for fun, such as fishing or picking fruit, were valuable, providing them with skills that could be useful well into adulthood.[15]

While much is made of medieval illiteracy, it was expected that children who could afford the materials and the time should learn how to read. In part, this was to ensure that they could access the Christian teachings that would allow their souls to be saved, but it was also considered foundational to any further education, and education—then, as now—paired with excellent manners could be the key to bettering your station. More than one powerful courtier had humble beginnings, and scholarships to university existed to set those who had aptitude on the path to success.

In the later Middle Ages especially, mothers often assumed responsibility for their children's early literacy, teaching them how to read in Latin as well as in their own language. Many books of hours feature the Virgin Mary's mother, Saint Anne, teaching Mary how to read or Mary teaching Jesus—appropriate illustrations for the children who were likewise learning their letters at their

*As well as being fashionable jewelry, signet rings were
pressed into hot wax to identify documents as authentically
from the sender, as with this early medieval example which
simply says, "of Mark" in Greek.*
Signet ring, c. 6th–7th century
Walters Art Museum, Baltimore

mothers' knees, using books of hours.[16] However, literacy for women might only include reading, not writing, a skill considered to be separate and not necessarily important, as long as there were others around to transcribe. As Geoffrey de la Tour Landry says:

> Some people say they don't want their wives and daughters to have any learning or to know how to write. I answer them that as for writing, it doesn't matter if a woman knows anything of it, but reading is good and profitable for all women. For a woman who can read may better know the perils of the soul and of her salvation than she who can't, and that's been proven.[17]

Many noble girls never studied formally beyond reading, but there were some exceptions, such as Christine de Pizan, whose father insisted on her being educated over the objections of her mother. Ever a champion of women's education, Pizan says, in the voice of Lady Reason, "If it were customary to send little girls to school and have them study the sciences as is customary for boys, they would learn and understand the subtleties of all the arts and sciences just as well as boys."[18] Regardless

Noble parents sometimes hired tutors to ensure that their children had a good, wide-ranging education. Here, the scholar Boethius teaches a boy arithmetic.
Liber Alchandrei Philosophi, fol. 26r, c. 1405 (detail)
Getty Museum, Los Angeles; MS 72

of their gender, if children's education was to continue at home, a tutor could be hired to teach some of the more complicated subjects, such as music, grammar, rhetoric, mathematics, or astronomy. What you knew, however, was rarely as important as who you knew and how well you learned your social niceties. For this reason, Pizan writes that it's important to choose a master who is "wise and prudent, more in manners than in great science."[19]

Sometime between ages seven and ten, children were sent to school at a monastery or cathedral if their parents believed they should pursue a career in the church. Boys destined to become knights left to be fostered, as we saw, while girls who were betrothed might join their future husbands' families to begin training as the next lady of the house. For young princesses, this might mean becoming trilingual, mastering an entirely different language in addition to their own and Latin, as well as learning foreign customs. Because of this regular movement of children, at the same time a noble husband and wife might have sent their own sons and daughters out into the world, they might well be accepting other people's children into their home.

Medieval parents could find themselves raising children who weren't biologically theirs for a variety of reasons. Fostering was a normal part of being a well-respected member of the aristocracy, but both aristocrats and those in the lower classes could be expected to have young servants or apprentices in their homes, as a large number of medieval teenagers worked as servants in order to save money and gain skills before marriage. High mortality rates—especially in childbirth—also meant a lot of families were blended, with stepmothers and stepfathers sometimes bringing stepchildren into a marriage. Blending families could be complicated for emotional as well as inheritance reasons, and the trope of the evil stepmother is one that has lasted for centuries in folk and fairy tales. (The "stepmother's slice" was what people called it when they received only a bit of bread.) La Tour Landry tells his daughters a woman "can't show her lord any greater love than to love his children from other women," suggesting that while raising other peo-

*When fathers died, mothers were often responsible for
supervising the care and the properties of their children,
even in the case of royalty.*

Des Cas des Nobles Hommes et Femmes, fol. 120r, c. 1413–15 (detail)
Getty Museum, Los Angeles; MS 63

ple's children was a normal part of life, it may have taken
extra effort to love them equally.[20]

Finally, orphaned children might be adopted by their
relatives or taken on as wards, whose welfare, wealth,
and lands would be in the hands of their caregivers until
they reached adulthood or were married. As with their
own children, lords could arrange marriages for their
wards, but abuse of this privilege led to English laws

specifically stating that these marriages were to benefit the ward, not the lord. English wards had the prerogative to refuse an arranged match; however, they would later have to financially compensate their guardians for the trouble.[21] Given that chivalric texts specifically call for the care of widows and orphans, guardians were both legally and honor bound to treat their wards well.

After age ten or twelve, raising children became much less about allowing play and more about preparing the next generation of adults. This meant, as we've seen, integrating them into the adult world with roles such as cupbearing or becoming ladies-in-waiting. Since these young men and women would someday be the ones in

Knights and ladies were raised to be good company: they learned how to dance and how to play games like chess.
Arthurian Romances, fol. 66v, c. 1290–1300 (detail)
Yale University Library, New Haven, CT; Beineke 229

charge of vast landholdings, it was important to nurture good relationships between them and nip any potential bad blood in the bud.

In addition to a noble family's own children and those they cared for as guardians, an aristocratic household could have anywhere from a dozen to well over a hundred servants, from cooks to shepherds, most of them teens and most of them male. A lord was responsible for ensuring that these young men didn't make trouble in his house or on his lands, and some lords took their duties of care further, with kings such as Edward II and Edward IV sending well-behaved boys from their households to study at Cambridge and Oxford to give them a higher education and better job prospects.[22] Evidently, good manners could indeed take a young man far.

The lady of the house was responsible for ensuring that every young woman under her roof was infinitely marriageable, from her skills as a chatelaine to her beauty, learning, and virtue. Christine de Pizan writes:

> [A good lady] will gladly read books teaching good morals and sometimes devotional books. She will detest books about dishonest and lubricious things and will not have them at her court and will not let them be brought before her daughter, relative, or lady-in-waiting, for there is no doubt that examples of good or evil influence the minds of those who see or hear them.[23]

Impressionability and naivete were considered especially dangerous in households in which dozens of handsome youths might have lived and worked. One medieval mother advises, "If thou have a daughter of age, / Pute here sone to maryage; / For meydens, thei be lonely" ("if you have a daughter of age, put her soon to marriage; for maidens, they will be lonely"), while the

*Christine de Pizan demonstrates a lady's responsibility to teach
her children how to be good and moral members of society, as she
instructs her reluctant son.*
Proverbes Moraux, fol. 261v, c. 1410–14 (detail)
British Library, London; Harley 4431

Goodman of Paris insists that caution extend to every
young lady in the house:

If you have girls or chambermaids from 15 to 20 years
old, who at that age are so foolish and have seen so little of the world, make them sleep near you in a dress-

ing room or chamber . . . where there is, of course, no dormer or low window onto the street.[24]

Although this is based, in part, on the assumption that young women are both foolish and—in the supposed way of all women—lusty, keeping them both safe and virginal in a houseful of adolescent boys was part of ensuring their futures at a time when evidence or even suspicion of premarital sex could ruin their marriage prospects. While a man might indulge in a youthful love affair with his reputation unscathed, a woman could not, especially if she became pregnant.[25] Preventing romantic liaisons between the young men and women in her care kept a lady's home free of both drama and scandal, as well as making certain there would be no unexpected little ones added to her charge.

Fundamentally, then as now, raising children is about ensuring that they have the skills and opportunities to become successful adults. From supplying them with toys and books to teaching them morality to allowing them to make friends to protecting them from harm, parents and guardians have an unparalleled ability to shape children into healthy, well-adjusted members of society, regardless of their place in it. Well-mannered children, as we've seen, had the potential to greatly improve their lives, whether through job or marriage prospects, so teaching them wisdom and courtesy was essential. Part of that teaching, of course, was by setting a good example.

Keep the Home Fires Burning

Medieval ladies are known for being kept at the top of towers, waiting for rescue, but in the real world they were the beating heart of the household, ensuring that everyone was fed and cared for in a way that brought honor upon their family names. In theory, it was a lord's job to manage everything found within his borders, including the domestic sphere, but in practice, men were often away, leaving everything from logistics and supervision to defense in the hands of their wives.[26]

One of the best sources for understanding the very practical duties expected of a wife is *Le Ménagier de Paris* (*The Goodman of Paris*), a fifteenth-century book written by an older husband for his fifteen-year-old bride. The Goodman wrote down everything he thought his wife should know in order to be a good spouse to him and to anyone she might marry after his death.[27] Although he declares, "You are hardly overburdened, and have only the obligations rightly belonging to you, which should be pleasant, such as serving God and taking care of your husband's person,"[28] the Goodman then proceeds to write well over a hundred pages in minute detail of the things she is to learn and remember.

The Goodman's wife, as a well-to-do Parisian woman of noble blood, "need only take on the command, the supervision, and the conscientiousness to have things done right, but have the work performed by others, at your husband's expense."[29] The trouble is, of course, that doing things "right" implies an in-depth awareness of every task necessary for the smooth and honorable running of the household, whether or not the wife performs it herself. As we saw, the "work performed by others" could include the jobs of dozens of servants, all of which the lady of the house needed to know well enough that she actually *could* perform them herself. One mother advises her daughter that it's wise to pitch in with her servants at times, "For many handes make lyght werke" ("many hands make light work").[30]

Though she might not be the one performing all of the domestic duties, a lady was required to know how to do each one, such as churning butter.
Arthurian Romances, fol. 300v, c. 1290–1300 (detail)
Yale University Library, New Haven, CT; Beineke 229

Part of a chatelaine's job was making sure that the household was well supplied. The most obvious necessities, of course, were food and water, and in a time before food was both plentiful and able to be imported into countries with a shorter growing season, this meant not only getting groceries for the week, but also figuring out how much was needed over the long winter months—and where to store it all. In a memorable letter from fifteenth-century England, Margaret Paston asks her husband to pick up some supplies while he is away, including almonds, sugar, broadcloth—and crossbows.[31] A woman instructing servants to pick up groceries or other supplies would need to provide them with specific instructions on where to go and what to get, and Margaret likewise helpfully suggests where John should

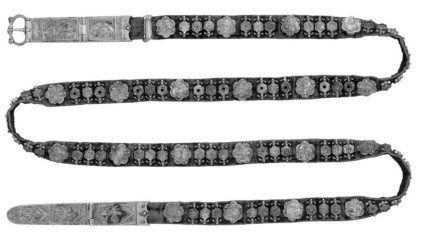

Belts were worn by everyone in medieval Europe and could be used to show off status, wealth, and cosmopolitanism, as well as being a handy place to keep keys.
Belt, c. 1330–50
The Met Cloisters, New York

get both the crossbows and some fabric for the children's clothes. To make such delegation easier on his wife, the Goodman lists all the best shops in Paris, the amount of food necessary for different special occasions, and recipes that he'd like her to become familiar with, ranging from quick sauces to desserts like candied orange peel, which take months to prepare.

In addition to knowing where to get the best items at the best prices, managing supplies also meant finding ways to prevent them from being pilfered, leading many women to keep expensive commodities like spices under lock and key, "to prevent waste and excess by the servants."[32] Large supplies of food, such as a that from a bountiful harvest, would have to be protected not only from thieves, but also from rodents, insects, mold, and mildew. The Goodman of Paris writes, "Should your household servants report that rats are spoiling your grain, bacon, cheese, and other provisions, tell [the steward] that he can kill rats in six ways," including using traps, poison, sponges, and of course, cats.[33] He also expects his lady to learn how to get rid of ants, fleas, caterpillars, and mosquitoes, so that she can pass this knowledge to the servants as needed.

While most perishable items would be produced within a lady's own landholdings, many essentials were not stockpiled but made-to-order, meaning that she needed to plan well in advance for upcoming events like the forty fish days of Lent, seasonal festivals, and family celebrations. If she was pregnant, she'd have to plan for everything to keep running smoothly while she was in her confinement, closed in her room for the last month of pregnancy and the six weeks after delivery, before she was "churched" and reintegrated into society.[34] (Fortunately, her female caregivers would be seeing to her own needs during this time.) A well-bred lady would also need contingency plans in place for the unexpected, such as crop failures, funerals, sieges, or unplanned visits from relatives—or even the king himself, who might drop by if he was in the neighborhood administering justice on royal progress.

Whether or not she was expecting guests, the chatelaine was responsible for making sure everyone in the house had sufficient blankets, sheets, and pillows, as well as the linens required for banquets and feasts. Fortunately, sheets and bedclothes were often bequeathed in wills, allowing some women to collect several sets of these pricey materials,[35] and table linens, as we've seen, could be rented. Other textiles that fell under the lady's purview were her own and her husband's everyday and seasonal clothing, as well as the clothing of the children, which would need more frequent washing and repair. After each use, the lady would need to arrange for textiles to be washed or aired out, then "brought inside, shaken out to remove most of the dust and then cleaned and beaten using dry sticks."[36] The Goodman of Paris, attentive to detail, even provides his wife with several handy stain-removal techniques.

In addition to fresh food and clean linen, it was essential for the woman in charge to keep a steady supply of many other household items required for everyday life in a time before electricity, such as candles, torches, lamps, and oil to light her home and outbuildings. She'd also need to keep an ample amount of firewood on hand to provide warmth and to heat water for cooking, cleaning, and bathing. Luckily, as we saw in chapter three, young squires and knights could be put to work chopping wood as part of their training—one of the many ways in which multitasking made medieval life efficient.

If she were wealthy enough, a lady would have a team of people to help manage her estate, each with their own experience and skill set. Her duty to her servants was to ensure they were "well fed . . . warm and comfortable," although never idle. Keeping servants busy was thought necessary to prevent them from making trouble, but a good lady knew it was just as important to make a point to recognize their efforts and boost their morale. As the Goodman says, "You, too, must display to your people that you oversee it all, are quite familiar with their work, and deem it important, for then they will be more diligent."[37]

In addition to knowing the ins and outs of every household chore, the duties of each servant, the present condition of all supplies, the price of a decent side of beef, and the sexual history of everyone under her roof, the

woman of the house was also meant to be knowledgeable about horse breeding, wolf poisons, pet food, hor-
ticulture, and medicinal cures. "In a nutshell," says the
Goodman, "that is all."[38]

To place all domestic chores under the purview of
women is an obviously outdated idea, especially when
women are also working outside the home. Built as it is
on ideas of universal submission to men, it's one worth
leaving behind in favor of an equal distribution of domestic work—something we are still working toward as
a society.

What we can learn from the organizational superpow-
ers of medieval women, however, is how valuable it is for
everyone in the household to understand what it takes to
run it on the daily—and to be capable of doing so—as well
as to plan for unexpected circumstances. While we may
not need to worry about spontaneous royal drop-ins these
days, climate change has made it necessary to prepare for
extreme weather events which may require us to lay in
the same basic supplies as a pre-electric medieval home:
water, food, and fuel. When everyone knows what to
do and how to do it, they'll be ready as a team to tackle
anything from daily chores to climate-related sieges.

Take Care of Business

While part of the business of a knight or lord was
directly serving the king on campaign or in
a council chamber, at home his job was to ensure the
smooth running of his landholdings, which involved
everything from signing off on apprenticeships to buying
and selling real estate. An unkind or neglectful lord would
have rebellions brewing in his house and on his land, so it
was the duty of a good one to facilitate everyone's work,
for their sake as well as his own.

Lords were responsible for the protection and well-being of all those who lived on their land, like these villagers attending a church service.
Book of hours, leaf, c. 1550 (detail)
Getty Museum, Los Angeles; MS 50

The biography of Marshal Boucicaut gives us a glimpse into what a lord's everyday life might have been like. After getting up "very early" to spend "three hours at prayer,"

> he attends his council, which lasts until dinner. After dinner, which he takes briskly and in public . . . he gives audience to all sorts of people who want to address him or ask him a favour. . . . He deals with each of them quickly and dispenses justice and favours rapidly. . . . Thereafter he withdraws to his study, and composes any letters he wishes to send, and issues orders to his people; after that, unless he is really too busy, he attends vespers. After vespers he works for a while, or talks to those who need his attention until he is ready to retire, at which point he will issue his last directions and go to bed.[39]

As this passage suggests, much of a lord's job was to hear advice and complaints and dispense both justice and favors. While he didn't have as much unbridled power as we may see in the movies (jus primae noctis, for example, is a myth), a lord did control the land on which his tenants farmed and traded, and he did have a say in who could go where and when, which meant that his decisions were important ones with far-reaching consequences that could sometimes mean the difference between life and death. That Boucicaut could make such decisions quickly and in a way that pleased everyone is a testament to his greatness as a lord—and the agenda

This lord receives a letter, but evidently does not write them himself, leaving his clerks to conduct the written part of his business.
Historia de Duobus Amantibus, fol. 23r, c. 1460–70 (detail)
Getty Museum, Los Angeles; MS 68

of his biographer. Lords didn't dispense justice alone—there was a complex system of courts, judges, and juries—but they did hear cases and mitigate disputes, especially about land.

Because his land was required to feed everyone on it, the lord needed to ensure that his tenants were farming it well and properly, and that anyone who couldn't do so was either supported or replaced. This was a matter of wealth, but also a matter of survival. A good lord was one who, like his lady, planned ahead for possible food shortages as well as outside threats. One enjoyable way to get a sense of how his land and people were faring was to go hunting. Niccolò Machiavelli says a good lord should

> be constantly engaged in the chase, that he may inure his body to hardships and fatigue, and gain at the same time a knowledge of places, by observing how the mountains slope, the valleys open, and the plains spread; acquainting himself with the characters of rivers and marshes, and giving the greatest attention to this subject. . . . [H]e learns thereby to know his own country, and to understand better how it may be defended.[40]

Hunting gave lords the opportunity to survey their domains, speak with their people, and plan for any trouble, all while keeping their martial skills sharp and catching dinner. No wonder it was a favorite aristocratic pastime.

Just as today, political rumblings were usually evident before they became outright conflicts, so a prudent lord could read the signs and ensure that his land and his people were prepared for any eventuality. When summoned to war, a lord was meant to bring a set number of equipped retainers with him and only had about a month to req-

Hunting was not only a sport, but a way to monitor the condition of the land and ensure that there was enough food on the table.

Livre de la Chasse, 81v, c. 1430–40 (detail)
Getty Museum, Los Angeles; MS 27

uisition and kit them out before they were expected to arrive at the muster point. This was too late to sufficiently train those who had never used a weapon before—given that they needed that month to get their affairs in order before marching—so it made sense to keep knights continually sharp and archers continually practicing. For fourteenth-century English lords, this was relatively easy, as Edward III had decreed that every man was to practice archery on Sundays, a skill that served them well during many battles of the Hundred Years' War.

In the event of a conflict on his own soil, the lord's home—his castle—became the refuge of his people, sheltering them for as long as it took for the threat to dissipate. While he was meant to depend on his king to send aid to lift a siege from outside the walls, the lord was responsible for everything that happened within the walls, and ultimately whether or not his people survived. Lords who abandoned their people in times of need were unpopular, indeed.

Although not usually ruled over directly by a lord, German towns were praised by Machiavelli for their preparedness in the event of a siege, giving us an idea of what sort of arrangements a lord might make in anticipation of one. This included everything from food to raw materials:

> All of [the towns] are protected by moats and suitable ramparts, are well supplied with artillery, and keep their public magazines constantly stored with victual, drink and fuel, enough to last them for a year. Besides which, in order to support the poorer class of citizens without loss, they lay in a common stock of materials for these to work on for a year, in the handicrafts which are the life and sinews of such cities, and by which the common people live. Moreover, they esteem military exercises and have many regulations for their maintenance.[41]

Preparedness allowed some castles to hold out for months and even years, despite ongoing conflicts, enabling the people inside to withstand fierce attacks, whether or not the lord was at home.

Part of the reason lords were required to be educated and refined as well as tough was their continual need to schmooze other nobles so that conflicts never came to a head in the first place. Medieval Europe was a place where everyone had to rely on interconnected and shared resources, from fields and forests to roads, bridges, waterways, and ports. As a lord, ensuring that you got all your rights, safe passage, and access to mills meant playing nicely with others. Sometimes this meant making a large donation to the local monastery to encourage the abbot to share his mill with the local villagers. Sometimes this meant marrying your child to the child of an enemy. Always, it involved a keen sense of local politics and an understanding of the current state of affairs both within and without your domain.

Very few of us today are actual lords responsible for entire estates or villages, but we may often find ourselves in leadership positions, where we are responsible for the welfare of others in ways both big and small. What we can learn from a good medieval lord is to listen to the opinions and advice of others, mitigate disputes in a way that ensures both parties feel heard and respected, and smooth over obstacles so that our people can do their best work. People in charge tend to be the ones who can see the big picture, so we look to them to plan ahead, protect our investments, and do what needs to be done to make everything run efficiently for the benefit of all.

Love the One You're With

Medieval marriage was, for all intents and purposes, an unbreakable bond, whether a person got into it for romantic, political, or survival reasons. On the day of their wedding, couples would take vows to forever love the person whose hands they held, and as we saw earlier, once the marriage was consummated, it was ride or die.

The ideal marriage in the Middle Ages was something straight out of a 1950s manual for housewives, involving creating "a paradise of relaxation" for husbands and "always plac[ing] his pleasure first."[42] The Goodman of Paris says:

Love your husband's person carefully . . . see that he
has clean linen, for that is your domain, while the concerns and troubles of men are those outside affairs
that they must handle, amidst coming and going, running here and there, in rain, wind, snow, and hail,
sometimes drenched, sometimes dry, now sweating,
now shivering, ill fed, ill lodged, ill shod, and poorly
rested. . . . Cheer him: removing his shoes in front of
a good fire, washing his feet, offering clean shoes and
socks, serving plenteous food and drink, respectfully
honoring him. . . . [Put] him to sleep in white sheets and
his nightcap, covered with good furs, and satisf[y] him
with other joys and amusements, intimacies, loves, and
secrets about which I remain silent. The next day . . . set
out fresh shirts and garments for him.[43]

A woman was meant to be obedient to her husband in
all things, even those that seemed arbitrary or silly, because it was believed a good husband would never ask his
wife to do anything untoward, and even if he did, it would
be worth it to please him.[44] Women were to be mindful of
their own greater tendency toward sin, and always aware
that they were "taken from man," as Genesis describes.

Obedience meant submission to the point of ignoring
infidelity, or even supporting it, since it was through
meek acceptance that a wife would eventually win her
husband back. The Goodman of Paris relates a story of a
wife who tracks down her husband's mistress and, seeing that she is poor, gives the mistress what she needs
to make her husband comfortable next time he visits.
After being treated so well by the mistress and discov-
ering the cause, the husband realizes what a good wife
he has and returns to her. (She accepts him back joyfully, of course.)[45]

This serving plate depicting a wife thrashing her husband would have been considered funny to medieval diners, as it shows the reversal of the "natural" hierarchy within the household.
Plate, c. 1480
The Met Cloisters, New York

Though women were meant to treat their husbands with this kind of self-effacing reverence, the unfairness of such expectations evidently did grate on them. In *The Book of the Three Virtues*, Christine de Pizan writes:

> Some ladies may say to us that we tell only one side of the story, saying that no matter what ladies must love their husbands and show it, but that we do not consider whether all husbands deserve this kind of treatment from their wives, for we all know that there are husbands who treat their wives atrociously and without any sign of love, or hardly any.

Unfortunately for these women, Pizan has bad news:

> If this is the case, there is nothing she can do about it. . . . [I]f you speak to him harshly, you will gain nothing . . . you would only kick against the spur:

he may leave you and people would mock you, adding shame and dishonor, and even worse things may happen. You must live and die with him, whatever he is like.[46]

Fortunately, some women found relief in the arms of their families, while others chose new partners regardless of what society had to say about it. The notorious Lucy de Thweng left her loveless marriage to live with another man for many years, even having children together, despite the objections of the church and some of her neighbors.[47]

Although adultery was a punishable sin for both sexes, men were similarly advised to ignore any affairs their wives may have been having. This wasn't chivalry, but an attempt to keep the peace within the household and—more importantly—to keep their reputations intact. Men were judged by other men for how well they "controlled" their wives, so it's understandable that they might have wanted to keep their wives' affairs to themselves unless something undeniable, like an ill-timed pregnancy, forced them to acknowledge the situation. Adultery was a much riskier business for women for this very reason, so it was not to be committed lightly, or at least not without learning about one of the many contraceptive recipes of the time.

While it's nearly impossible to talk about medieval marriage without the specter of adultery, given the extreme popularity of courtly love themes in story and song, this doesn't mean that couples never loved each other or never tried to make things work. Most medieval commentary on marriage is either sermonizing or satire, so a large part of the extant medieval works on marriage involve unhappy ones, usually those in which the wife is in the wrong. It can be difficult to know from such

In many medieval stories and jokes, marital relationships are
depicted as adversarial, as in this marginal illustration in which
a woman jousts with her distaff.
Arthurian Romances, fol. 329r, c. 1290–1300 (detail)
Yale University Library, New Haven, CT; Beineke 229

sources what a good marriage looked like, but there are
some surviving texts that give us clues.

In the Middle English poem *How the Goode Man
Taght Hys Sone* (*How the Good Man Taught His Son*), the
father says:

> . . . sone, yf thou wylt have a wyfe,
> Take hur for no covetyse,
> But loke, sone, sche be thee lefe . . .
>
> For bettry hyt ys in reste and pees,
> A messe of potage and no more,
> Then for to have a thousand messe
> Wyth grete dysese and anger sore.
>
> . . . son, if you will have a wife,
> Don't take her out of greed [for wealth]
> But make sure, son, she is loved by you. . . .
>
> For it is better, in rest and peace,
> [To have] a meal of pottage and nothing else
> Than to have a thousand meals
> With great dis-ease [unease] and sore anger.[48]

Courtly love dictated that knights were meant to be subservient to their ladies, as depicted in this gemellion (washbowl), but a truly successful marriage depended on compatibility and partnership.
Gemellion, c. 1250–1300
Walters Art Museum, Baltimore

Although this father has the power to steer his son toward a woman who might enrich the family name and fortunes, instead he encourages his son to choose based on feelings and compatibility. It's unclear whether the father's words come from his own experience, but his advice reminds us that marriage is much more than a dowry.

Perhaps, following this advice, the father's son turned into a man like John Paston, who in 1477 received a letter from his beloved, Margery Brews, calling him her "right well-beloved Valentine." Margery was writing John with some bad news: her father would not increase her dowry despite her, and her mother's, efforts. "But if you love me," she writes, "as I trust verily that you do, you will not leave me therefore." John was true to Margery, marrying her despite her unsatisfactory dowry, and we can hope Margery was likewise true to her word when she said, "My heart me bids evermore to love you truly over all earthly things."[49]

As the father above suggests, it's important for both spouses to pull together to make things work. He says, "work with your wife" ("Wyrche with thy wife") because "though she is a servant to some degree / To some degree she is your fellow [equal]" ("Thogh sche be sirvunt in degree, / In some degre sche fellowe ys"). The father is not outright disagreeing with the church's take on where husbands and wives stand in relation to each other, but at the same time, he points out that women do, indeed, have important insights worth hearing. While he knows it will be his son's responsibility to chastise his wife if she is in the wrong, in his experience, he says, men with quick tempers often have wives who act out because of it.[50] Treating women respectfully is not only more chivalrous, but it also makes for a happier home.

Although Marie de Champagne, Andreas Capellanus's authority on fin' amors, is said to have decreed, "love can exert no power between husband and wife,"[51] Christine de Pizan was one woman who found love and joy in her marriage, declaring,

> I was above all honored by him into whose keeping I had been given, who worked very hard for me so that, experiencing no difficulties, I felt very comfortable.... And he was so faithful to me, and so good that, by my soul, I could not praise highly enough the good things that I received from him. He was handsome and good under all circumstances, wise, courtly and upright, and he greatly valued nobility and learning.[52]

Pizan's beloved husband died young, and though she struggled to get by on her own, like many medieval widows she never remarried.

Despite being the ones with the most temporal power in medieval Europe, royals had little personal agency over whom they married, given that the future of the kingdom frequently weighed in the balance. And yet,

Christine de Pizan (in blue) rides along with nobles who are using the opportunity to flirt.
Le Livre des III Jugements, fol. 81r, c. 1410–14 (detail)
British Library, London; Harley 4431

even in these arranged marriages, true love could sometimes be found. Edward I married Eleanor of Castile when they were both teenagers, and the two were nearly inseparable—except for the brief period when Edward's father, Henry III, did separate them for being too much in love. For his part, Henry III also cared deeply for his queen, Eleanor of Provence. Although Richard II's mar-

Though royal unions were frequently arranged by parties other than the bride and groom, they could result in loving, supportive marriages.
Romance of the Three Kings' Sons, fol. 9r, c. 1475–85 (detail)
British Library, London; Harley 326

riage to Anne of Bohemia was brief—she died of the plague after twelve years by his side—he grieved her loss deeply. Edward IV stood by the wife he chose, Elizabeth Woodville, instead of bowing to pressure to put her aside and marry someone who could bring a continental alliance to the realm.[53]

Dowry or no dowry, kingdom or no kingdom, who you choose as a romantic partner can be instrumental to your success, whether you're together for a little while or for life. For medieval people, loving the one you were with meant making the best of a marriage, even a bad one. Luckily for us, in the modern world loving the one we're with can mean giving extra affection and emotional support to our partners, or—if we discover we truly are no longer in love—caring enough to gently let go.

Running a household is a big task: there may be children to raise and a relationship to nurture, and there will always be work and domestic chores. The best way to manage it all is to show others courtesy amid the chaos, whether that's through taking on an equal share of chores or childcare, working in a way that is supportive and uplifting, or making sure we show our partners the love they deserve.

HOW TO RULE A KINGDOM

If you are a ruler of kingdoms, a sovereign on earth,
govern your subjects so carefully that no grave mistake
born from the flightiness of your mind can do them harm.
—Daniel of Beccles, *The Book of the Civilised Man*

To succeed at ruling a kingdom requires being well-versed in everything we've looked at so far: a good ruler has great table manners, knows how to treat their partner well, can fight should the need arise, and can care for their home and lands with skill. But a great ruler can take these skills and run with them so that they are remembered long after they're gone.

Level Up

Whether they were born to govern or inherited a kingdom on the death of a relative, a medieval ruler couldn't fully reign until they'd leveled up by means of a coronation. Today, a coronation might seem like a formality, solidifying the rule of someone who's already had the power of the monarchy vested in them. In the Middle Ages, however, a sovereign wasn't a sovereign until they were endorsed by God. When Henry I of England died in 1135, his nephew Stephen raced to Westminster

Books of advice—called mirrors for princes—were often given to kings as gifts alongside tales of chivalry.
Presentation scene, fol. 2v, c. 1444–45 (detail)
British Library, London; Royal 15 E VI

Royal marriages were almost always political, meant to form alliances and unite kingdoms. The marriage of Ferdinand II and Isabella, pictured on this coin, united much of what is Spain today.

Spanish coin (obverse), c. 16th century
National Gallery of Art, Washington, DC

Abbey to get himself crowned before the rightful heir—Henry's daughter Matilda—could. This threw England into a nineteen-year civil war called the Anarchy, all because of a vial of holy oil.

Unlike in many modern countries, there was no separation of church and state in the Middle Ages—quite the opposite. Although kings and popes wrestled over power and jurisdiction, the pope was grudgingly accepted as the most powerful person on earth, in part because kingship was not considered wholly valid without the blessings performed at the coronation, and that depended on the church. (Checkmate.)

In the coronation ceremony, an archbishop anointed the new king on the forehead and chest with holy oil (chrism) in the shape of the cross, giving him God's blessing to rule over the people. The archbishop then placed the crown on the head of the king and gave him the scepter and orb representing earthly and heavenly power over the (spherical) earth, as well as an increasing collection of other symbolic objects, including a ring, mantle, and spurs. From that moment, the king became more than human: he was chosen by God and endowed with the divine right to rule. After Stephen had been anointed, it's easy to see how Matilda's queenship became a tough sell.

While the coronation ceremony made kings more powerful than they had been the day before, there were other ways for rulers to level up their game. A classic move was to marry into power, gaining a spouse with a formidable family to back you in times of crisis or with plenty of land to help expand your territory. When Eleanor of Aquitaine married Henry II, she effectively doubled Henry's landholdings on the continent, much to the chagrin of the French king, Louis VII, her previous husband.[1]

Although kings routinely married for land or alliances, some royal relationships were more successful than others. When Edward I of England, having had a happy and successful arranged marriage, wed his son to a French princess, he looked forward to a healthy alliance that would strengthen both kingdoms. Instead, Isabella used her French connections to overthrow her husband, installing their son, Edward III, in his place.

Despite the uncomfortable start to his reign, Edward III became a master of leveling up his own royal game through chivalry; that is, by winning battles. Through his formidable mother's lineage, Edward claimed that he was the true heir to the throne of France as well as England, and his determination to rule both was the impetus for the Hundred Years' War. While we in the modern world might not consider starting a century-long

Jousting was a popular sport for royals as well as nobles,
increasing their skills for mounted combat.
Codex Manesse, fol. 52r, c. 1300–40 (detail)
Heidelberg University Library, Germany; Cod. Pal. German 848

conflict an admirable move for a leader, for a medieval
king like Edward, war was a road to glory. England's
series of wins under his leadership included some of

Le Jouvencel, *a thinly veiled autobiography by Jean
de Bueil, provided its audience with an entertaining
story and instruction on how to be a good knight. Here,
Jouvencel is seen examining prisoners of war.*
Le Jouvencel, fol. 173v, c. 1450–99 (detail)
British Library, London; Royal 16 F I

the most storied battles of his age: Sluys, Crécy, and
Poitiers. Winning battles kept his country happy—
England, that is, not France, whose countryside he rav-
aged in the process—giving his rule a stability not guar-
anteed when he usurped the throne.

It's evident that Edward III was a king who took chivalry seriously; he was, after all, the one who created the
Order of the Garter in imitation of King Arthur's knights
of the Round Table. Linking current knights with legendary ones added a veneer of heroism to the Hundred Years'
War, elevating it beyond a vicious fight over territory.

Old ideas of honor among the aristocracy meant that
nobles, and sometimes even commoners, could expect
to be ransomed if captured, which made even the bloody
business of war more palatable. When Henry V changed
the rules, killing his prisoners at Agincourt, it was a blow

to the collective psyche of the chivalric elite.[2] What Henry lost in chivalric reputation, however, he made up for in prowess, conquering France to the point that he became both regent and heir to the French throne. Though he accomplished it in a way that Machiavelli himself would have applauded, Henry V had persevered and leveled up through battle to become a king twice over.

It's unlikely any of us will be anointed and crowned in one kingdom, let alone two, but we will find ourselves fighting for a cause. It might be easier to relinquish our ideals in the press of battle or to change the rules in the middle of the game—sometimes you win that way. But it's better to gain allies and stick to your values, as in the end, Machiavelli says, "They who come to the Princedom . . . by virtuous paths, acquire with difficulty, but keep with ease."[3] People have more respect for someone who deserves to be where they are by having followed the rules. Henry V, as it happens, was embarrassed by the fact that his own father had taken the English crown by force, and Stephen never did win the hearts of his whole kingdom despite the holy chrism that made him king. For the virtuous, "all their difficulties are on the road, and may be overcome by courage."[4] The courage to take the harder, more honorable path, an ideal at the very heart of chivalry, will allow us to level up and achieve the highest heights.

Stack the Deck

They say that no man is an island, and this was still true of semidivine medieval kings, who were never able to rest securely on their thrones without powerful people supporting them. "The readiest conjecture we can form of the character and sagacity of a Prince," says Machiavelli, "is from seeing what sort of men he has about him."[5] In other words, it's important to surround yourself with good people.

While Edward II might not have thought it when he was being overthrown by his son, having heirs was the best way to solidify your position as king. No kingdom was secure without a prince to inherit, and the more heirs, the better. Every royal child represented a potential new alliance with a powerful family or state, as well as a better chance that the family dynasty would endure. The reason Henry I's death threw the kingdom into the Anarchy was because he only had one male heir, William Ætheling, who had drowned in the legendary sinking of the White Ship, along with many of England's aristocrats.

Fortunately for Henry—although perhaps not for his wives—while he had a dearth of legitimate heirs, he also had a whole host of illegitimate ones (twenty-three children in all) whom he placed in positions of power in another classic kingly move. Despite Henry's best efforts on his daughter's behalf, nothing could shift Stephen from the throne once he had sat upon it. Matilda's steadfast support from influential peers, however, allowed her to end the Anarchy by negotiating that her son would inherit instead of Stephen's. Henry II became king in 1154.

Another example of building power through family connections is that of the Woodvilles, the family of Elizabeth Woodville, who (as we saw in chapter two) became queen of England in a secret marriage ceremony to Edward IV. Over time, the Woodvilles were endowed with many of the most important positions and marriages in Edward's court, making them extremely powerful and extremely loathed. On Edward's death, his brother usurped the throne to become Richard III, taking his revenge on the Woodvilles by throwing the legitimacy

This miniature of the marriage of Edward IV to Elizabeth
Woodville shows many witnesses in attendance. In reality,
though, their marriage was conducted secretly, an event that
allowed detractors like the future Richard III to cast doubt on
its validity.

Anciennes chroniques d'Angleterre, fol. 109 (detail)
Bibliothèque Nationale de France, Paris; Français 85

of Edward's children into question, killing Elizabeth's
brother Earl Rivers, and possibly even murdering his own
nephews, better known to history as the Princes in the
Tower. But when Richard was killed at the Battle of Bo-
sworth, his niece Elizabeth of York became queen by marrying Henry Tudor, thereby ending the Wars of the Roses
and leaving a Woodville queen once again on the throne.

Other attempts to stack the deck with allies were less successful, as with Edward II, whose favorites were always despised and sometimes disemboweled, and Henry II, whose appointee to the archbishopric of Canterbury famously ended in disaster. Hoping to strengthen his position by placing a friend in the highest ecclesiastical seat in the realm, Henry installed his party pal Thomas Becket as archbishop. Unfortunately for Henry, once there, Thomas refused to bend to his will, causing a frustrating stalemate between the two men. In a rash outburst, Henry is said to have uttered, "Will no one rid me of this turbulent priest?" At which point some of his knights did just that and murdered Thomas in Canterbury Cathedral, gaining him a martyrdom and mightily compounding Henry's problems. In the end, Henry was forced to do penance on his knees at the cathedral while being whipped by monks. Thomas became a saint.[6]

On the other hand, Henry wisely took into his service the man who was said to be England's greatest knight, William Marshal. At first a retainer of Henry's son, the Young King, William would serve under three more English kings (Richard I, John, and Henry III), supporting them in war and peace, protecting John in the face of rebellion, and safeguarding the interests of the infant Henry III until his own death in 1219. William was one of the few people to take John's side during his barons' uprisings, despite John's best efforts to alienate him; he remained a steadying force in a tumultuous time.

Choosing councillors wisely was a fundamental part of kingship, as these men were meant to give the king good advice, support him financially and militarily, and tell him hard truths. Jean de Bueil, author of Le Jouvencel, has his titular character and the wisest of the leaders in the book take counsel whenever they make a decision.

Knights swore to serve and protect their kings in times
of difficulty, no matter how they might have felt about
royal policies.
Arthurian Romances, fol. 267r, c. 1290–1300 (detail)
Yale University Library, New Haven, CT; Beineke 229

"Princes and leaders of men," he says, "can do no better than to listen to advice." While having good councillors doesn't always mean a ruler or commander
will make the right decision in the end, collecting the
most knowledgeable people together and getting their
take on a situation is better than going it alone. Bueil
continues:

> A general council is better informed than one or two
> trusted advisers. . . . A prince therefore should never
> make major decisions as to action in private, but rather
> deliberate his great matters in a full council, and be
> advised by it—all the more so when a decision is to be
> made about something so crucial as a battle.[7]

Machiavelli agrees on the wisdom of good people, but clarifies that a ruler should not tolerate unsolicited advice:

A Prince . . . ought always to take counsel, but at such times and seasons only as he himself pleases, and not when it pleases others; nay, he should discourage everyone from obtruding advice on matters on which it is not sought. But he should be free in asking advice, and afterwards a patient hearer of the truth, and even displeased should he perceive that any one, from whatever motive, keeps it back.[8]

Like Bueil, Machiavelli also warns against listening to just one or two people. True to form, he puts his opinions on advisers bluntly:

It is an unerring rule and of universal application that a Prince who is not wise himself cannot be well advised by others, unless by chance he surrender himself to be wholly governed by some one adviser who happens to be supremely prudent; in which case he may, indeed, be well advised; but not for long, since such an adviser will soon deprive him of his Government.[9]

Cynicism aside, it's important for everyone to have reliable people in their lives they can count on for support and advice. While nepotism is generally frowned upon in this day and age, surrounding yourself with family outside of work, and friends both at and outside of work, can make it easier to see even the toughest problems more clearly. A wealth of perspectives makes for better decision-making, provided that the individual eventually does make a decision, instead of just getting stuck listening to endless advice.

Be a Good Kisser

K issing was a vital part of medieval culture, and not just for those who were romantically involved. It meant connecting intimately with one another and exchanging goodwill or devotion in platonic and even political relationships. People were often welcomed with a kiss, as when pilgrims or guests arrived at monasteries and were greeted by the abbot and the brothers. Saint Benedict believed that guests' sincerity should be tested before such courtesy and trust were extended, however: "The kiss of peace should not be offered until [a] prayer is finished," he writes, "because of diabolical trickery."[10]

Christians often kissed devotional objects as well as people to imbue themselves with divine blessing or to show the depth of their feeling. Philip Augustus's son Louis was healed of a grievous sickness, it was said, by kissing a few important relics, such as a nail from Jesus's crucifixion and the Crown of Thorns.[11] Medieval manuscripts, and even birth girdles, show a lot of wear on holy illustrations due to this very physical form of piety.[12]

When a new king was crowned, kissing was an important aspect of establishing bonds of fealty, to demonstrate to all who witnessed that both parties were on the same team and that no one was going to make trouble. One by one, each person would kneel before the king and swear his fealty to him, holding his hands in prayer position. The king would take the vassal's hands between his own and accept the pledge, and then the two would exchange a kiss of peace to seal the deal.

In his *Chronicles*, Jean Froissart describes the people of England renewing their homage to Richard II when he came of age at twenty-one, in order to solidify their bonds with him:

After mass the King's uncles kissed the King in sign of homage as his vassals and fief-holders, swearing perpetual allegiance to him. Next the earls and barons took the same oath and also the prelates and his dependent land-holders. They did homage in the customary way, with their hands clasped, kissing the King on the lips.[13]

This was a lot of kissing, and, like pressing their lips to a holy object, this was the closest most people would ever come to touching the divine in the flesh.

For rulers, kissing was serious business. They kissed visiting dignitaries, ambassadors, fellow royals, and even enemies. After a long and bitter dispute, a king might find himself having to exchange the kiss of peace with someone he detested. To seal peace with a kiss is to get up close and personal, not to mention extremely vulnerable, with an enemy, which makes it a dramatic display of trust.[14]

Knights—and even kings— were obliged to swear oaths of fealty to their overlords, as King Mark (left) does here with King Arthur.

Jeanne de Montbaston (active 1320–55), *Roman du Bon Chevalier Tristan, Fils au Bon Roy Meliadus de Leonois*, fol. 366r, c. 1320–40 (detail) Getty Museum, Los Angeles; Ludwig XV 5

Although this intimate contact was meant to wipe out all animosity, Richard's mixed acceptance of fealty demonstrates that this was not always the case:

> It was easy to see by watching this ceremony which ones the King kissed readily and which not. Although he kissed them, they were not all to his liking; but he had to go through with it.[15]

For those concerned about the most courteous way to kiss someone, *The Book of the Civilised Man* has some helpful advice:

> If you are about to be kissed, make sure that your
>   nostrils are clean,
> for mucus and spittle often leak from those openings.
> This is why one should be careful not to eat pungent
>   things in the market or the street.[16]

Luckily, chewing on cloves was a good medieval way to freshen up first.

For sovereigns, however, kissing was more about timing than technique. Knowing when to make your enemies submit and when to agree to a kiss of peace was essential. Although war could make a king very popular and respected, it was expensive in terms of time, money, and human life. While medieval history is often presented as a thousand years of continual conflict, in reality peace was always the goal.

After witnessing the Hundred Years' War bringing ruin to France for decades, Christine de Pizan, a prominent advocate for peace, wrote:

> It is never trivial to undertake a new war which should never be started without careful thought and serious

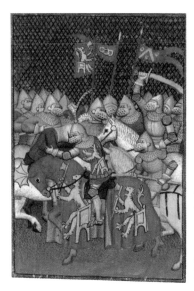

Though a king might gain a mighty reputation by winning battles, war was a costly activity. This illustration shows ancient Greek hero Achilles reimagined as a knight in contemporary armor, a reminder of both a lengthy and legendary war.
L'Épître Othéa, fol. 137r,
c. 1410–14 (detail)
British Library, London; Harley 4431

deliberations; and it would be better to think about a better way to reach an agreement by any fair means.[17]

A good king was willing to suppress his enmity to ensure peace, even if it meant embracing a hated rival. If he wasn't, it was time for his queen to step in.

Medieval queens should never be underestimated. Often trilingual, savvy, and raised in the heart of regal power, the queens of the Middle Ages used their wisdom, experience, statecraft, and alliances to influence the way their husbands and sons ruled. Much of the time, this was done subtly and behind the scenes, especially because "foreign" queens could be viewed with suspicion if they made their views too plain. When a queen did step to the fore, it was often in the role of intercessor, a worthy position for a woman in a time when the Virgin Mary herself was thought to play this role in heavenly matters. In her advice to princesses, Pizan says:

Women should especially devote themselves to peace, for men are by nature more courageous and hot-blooded, and their great desire for vengeance keeps them from considering the dangers and evils that can come from it. But woman's nature is more timid and of sweeter disposition, and therefore, if she is willing and wise, she can be the best means to pacify any man.[18]

Though a king could not be seen to relent to the pleas of people who were in his bad books, he could bend to the wishes of his queen, ostensibly out of love for her, without losing face.

The most famous instance of this, perhaps, occurred when Edward III besieged the city of Calais, whose citizens refused to accept his claim to the French throne. After eleven months of starvation and dire conditions, six townsmen—burghers—emerged from the city with ropes around their necks and the keys to the city in hand, ready to take on Edward's wrath if he would spare the city as it surrendered. At this moment, a strong king would make an example of these citizens for daring to defy him for so long, ensuring that other cities would heed the warning and surrender quickly. At the same time, everyone knew that killing six important and unarmed citizens would not endear Edward to the rest of Calais, nor to the other citizens of France, who might well decide never to surrender. Into the breach stepped Edward's queen, Philippa of Hainault:

The noble Queen of England, pregnant as she was, humbly threw herself on her knees before the King and said, weeping: "Ah, my dear lord, since I crossed the sea at great danger to myself, you know that I have never asked a single favour from you. But now I ask

The story of the Burghers of Calais is both moving and memorable, especially as captured by sculptor Auguste Rodin.
Auguste Rodin (1840–1917), *The Burghers of Calais*, c. 1884–95
Place du Soldat Inconnu, Calais, France

you in all humility . . . by the love you bear me, to have mercy on these six men."

Froissart says Edward's "heart was softened," and he handed the burghers into Philippa's keeping.[19] Whether or not she truly cared about the fate of these men, her intercession allowed Edward to show both power and mercy and to strengthen his reputation as a good husband at the same time, something that as a master of statecraft in her own right, Philippa knew very well. It was a win-win.

No matter who you're kissing, knowing when it's time to make peace with the people you interact with on a daily basis will help your life run more smoothly. While coming to terms with someone you actively dislike can leave a bad taste in your mouth, it may help you let go of any lingering animosity, turn an enemy into an ally, and set you on a path toward conquering your most ambitious goals.

Razzle-Dazzle 'Em

I n addition to being good kissers, kings had to look the part. One of the assets every ruler had going for them, Machiavelli insists, was "the majesty of the throne."[20] Majesty was not just about bloodlines, but about demonstrating to the world that you were a valuable and divinely blessed human being worthy of obedience. The more ordinary a monarch appeared, the less respected they were. To keep a rein on his reign, a king needed to look kingly.

Dressing to impress was especially important when royals and their retinues had similar names and were liable to be given sobriquets. Robert Curthose is just one example of a princely style icon, while the entire Plantagenet dynasty gets its name from *planta genista*, the flower worn in the hat of Henry II's father, Geoffrey of Anjou.

The most obvious symbol of royalty is, of course, the crown, but kings and queens didn't wear their coronation crowns all the time. While on ordinary days, a circlet or diadem would do, the big crowns would come out on special occasions, such as Christmas and Easter—important feasts when the royals were seen by more people than usual. Sovereigns might also wear their crowns when they needed to emphasize their station, such as when Richard the Lionheart returned to England after a long absence as both crusader and captive.[21] While a king might not wear his crown on a daily basis, there was never any doubt when looking at him that he was the king.

It was expected that the royal family would wear the most precious jewels, and many of these, like pearls, were sewn directly into their garments. They wore the most fashionable fabrics as well, including silks colored with expensive dyes and embroidered heavily with gold thread. We know that they wore ermine, in part because we can see it clearly in medieval art and in part because we have surviving formal dress codes—sumptuary laws—that say outright that they didn't want anyone else to wear it.

Unlike her husband, who was said to be fond of digging ditches, Isabella of France was criticized for her love of fashion and the amount she spent on it. While her son Edward III was not such a fashionista, it was he who imposed sumptuary laws that prohibited the English commons from dressing too much like their betters. In 1363, Edward issued a statute "Regarding the outrageous and excessive apparel of diverse people, violating their estate and degree, to the great destruction and impoverishment of the whole land." While this seems a little hysterical, it emphasizes how important it was that only their majesties should look majestic. People at the lowest end of the social spectrum were prohibited from wearing silver or silk, while those at the highest "shall wear what they like, except ermin and lettice [another expensive white fur], and apparel with jewels and pearls, unless on their heads."²² Luckily for those of all ranks, textiles could be created in a wide variety of colors using simple plant dyes, so no one needed to look particularly drab.

Being a sumptuous clotheshorse served royals in a second way, as they could gain even more prestige by passing down their

When even common people could afford exotic items like this beautifully carved and embellished coconut cup, kings needed to surround themselves with spectacular objects in order to radiate majesty.
Cup with cover, 1533/34
The Met Cloisters, New York

*Looking like a king was an
essential part of being a king.
Here, Louis XII's gold tunic
grants him the same ethereal
shine as Saints Michael,
Charles, Louis, and Denis.*
Jean Bourdichon (1457–1521),
Hours of Louis XII, leaf,
c. 1498–99 (detail)
Getty Museum, Los Angeles; MS 79a

regal castoffs. Many times, royal clothes were repurposed into liturgical vestments or other church textiles, while at other times, they were given to the less fortunate—or even entertainers.

We learn from Philip Augustus's monastic biographer that,

> Throngs of entertainers often gather in the courts of kings or other nobles, where they are accustomed to compete in the production of merriment . . . in order to obtain from these nobles gold, silver, horses, or the garments which nobles are accustomed to change frequently. . . . [C]ertain nobles, as soon as they were asked, gave to minstrels—that is, minions of the devil—garments of deep design and most skillful workmanship . . . for which they had paid twenty or thirty marks of silver and had hardly used for even seven days. For shame! Surely for the price of these

Colorful plant dyes gave people of all ranks the opportunity to step out in style.
Codex Manesse, fol. 166v,
c. 1300–40 (detail)
Heidelberg University Library,
Germany; Cod. Pal. German 848

garments twenty or thirty poor people could have been fed for the whole year. But the most Christian King Philip Augustus . . . remembered . . . that to give to entertainers is to make sacrifice to devils. . . . [H]e promised that as long as he lived . . . he would bestow his own garments upon the poor.[23]

It seems the starving artists of Philip's court were destined to remain unfashionable, too.

Arraying yourself and your household in a fabulous wardrobe wasn't just about looking good: it was also a way of showing that the realm was healthy and wealthy and that its ruler was generous. Machiavelli says, "To have credit for liberality with the world at large, you must neglect no circumstance of sumptuous display." This should extend, he explains, "at suitable seasons of the year to entertain the people with festivals and shows."[24]

As knights in their own right, kings might take time off from their administrative work to watch, or even participate in, tournaments.
Vidal Mayor, fol. 255r, c. 1290–1310 (detail)
Getty Museum, Los Angeles; Ludwig XIV 6

Generosity, or largesse, was a pillar of medieval courtesy, so a good ruler was always ready to give with an open hand, rewarding those who served well and impressing the common people every once in a while. In addition to festivals and shows, lavish celebrations and processions, rulers could impress their subjects in long-term ways as well, by founding colleges or monasteries or undertaking building works. Philip Augustus is remembered as the man behind the paving of Paris's streets, "a very difficult but quite necessary project," reportedly because he could not stand the smell of the mud.[25] If paving an entire city was not in the budget, a surefire way to impress the commoners was by supplying a wine fountain instead.

Dressing for the role you want, as we discussed in chapter two, is well and good, and doing so can take a person far. To make a truly memorable impression, however, is to understand the power of showmanship and to use it effectively, whether it's through your person or through your actions. In the words of Louis of Sancerre, elite French knight, "win or lose, do it with style."[26]

Hear Here

Fashionable dress was not only useful in impressing the nobles that the monarch saw on a day-to-day basis, but also in consolidating an image of power and glory for the common people when the royal family went on progress through the countryside. In administering justice to the whole kingdom, it was necessary for rulers to occasionally tour their domains to make appearances, check in on important members of society, and hear legal cases. While royal justice didn't extend to all crimes—offenses like adultery, bigamy, and heresy fell under the jurisdiction of the

It was the king's responsibility to provide justice and wisdom to his people, which meant spending a lifetime learning how to rule well.
Arthurian Romances, fol. 154v, c. 1290–1300 (detail)
Yale University Library, New Haven, CT; Beineke 229

*King John was frequently on the move, visiting
the towns and castles of his realm.*
Portrait of King John hunting, fol. 116r, c. 1300–99 (detail)
British Library, London; Cotton Claudius D II

church—those we still think of as major crimes, such as
murder, theft, and sexual assault, were in the sovereign's
purview. Those on the lower rungs of society had their
cases brought before lesser lords, but the aristocracy relied
upon the higher judgment of the king. Every free person
also had the right to appeal to the sovereign if they felt they
had been treated unfairly by their overlords, which is why
there will sometimes be a record of a king ruling in favor of
a commoner, for example.

Believe it or not, when royals went on progress, they
not only brought servants, clothing, and provisions
with them, but also took their own furniture. Medieval
architecture tended toward square or rectangular rooms
without a lot of built-in cupboards or shelves. Instead,
people had multipurpose and multifunctional furniture, including foldable chairs, trestle tables, and chests
galore. This meant that no matter where he stayed, the
king could use his own cup, his own chair, and his own
bedding. King John even brought his personal bathtub

with him on progress, cared for by an attendant named William. All of these royal objects were, like his clothing, meant to impress upon the people the vast wealth, glory, and power of the king. Bringing along these expensive goods was a necessary but sometimes risky venture, as John discovered when the tide came in too quickly during one of his journeys, leading to the crown jewels being swept out to sea.

Because a sovereign's hold over his people was rooted in land, kings were keenly invested in property rights, which is one of the reasons they went on progress: they could see exactly what was happening in their country with their own eyes. This was a helpful way for those who didn't live in and around the capital to get to know their ruler as well, making them more inclined to support him in times of unrest. As Machiavelli says, "It is essential for a Prince to be on a friendly footing with his people, since, otherwise, he will have no resource in adversity."[27] Travel also meant that royals could enjoy the vast swaths of land—or king's forests—that were reserved for their personal use in hunting and hawking, a pleasure not only for them, but for those locals deigned worthy enough to accompany them on such outings.

In addition to impressing the little people, a king hearing peasant's cases helped him to understand their concerns. Of course, very few people were permitted to give the king straight talk, and pretty much none of those people were commoners. But in administering justice, the king became involved in ordinary people's lives. It was a mark of honor and respect for the king to drop in on your town or stay the night at your house, even if it did make quite a lot of work for a host.

Although Machiavelli was writing hundreds of years after the reign of King John and in another country altogether, the two might have agreed on one point: whether

The Magna Carta was the result of rebellion against the tyrannical rule of King John. In it, he is forced to swear to uphold the law and preserve the rights of his people, especially the nobility.

Magna Carta, 1297 (detail)
National Archives,
Washington, DC

or not you're actually interested in people's welfare, it's important to seem as if you are.[28] John went on progress more often than most English kings, yet if he had been truly listening to his people, it's unlikely that he would have faced the wrath of his barons and been forced to concede to their demands, putting his seal to the Magna Carta in 1215.[29] Appearing to listen to the will of the people served John's descendant Richard II well when he rode out to meet the rebels during the Peasants' Revolt in 1381, dispersing most of the gathered mob peacefully. Like his ancestor, however, the teenage Richard turned out to be a fair-weather friend, punishing the rebels severely once the immediate danger had passed.

Modern politicians have mastered this trick of gracing villages, town halls, and even factories with their presence, making a show of how closely they're listening to the concerns of the people. Speaking to the average voter is a classic photo op, bound to tug on the heartstrings of regional and national pride. They understand the impact of hearing *here* is much greater than just saying you're listening from a distance.

Of course, hearing people's concerns is an act of love and care, which is why it's so effective in generating good feelings regardless of the sincerity of the listener. For people who genuinely want to lead with respect and compassion, being available to the people you serve is the best way to find out what they're thinking so you can meet

Since kings could not expect to be spared by the Wheel of Fortune, they were wise to conduct themselves as if they might lose everything.
Consolation de Philosophie, fol. 1v, c. 1460–70 (detail)
Getty Museum, Los Angeles; MS 42

their needs. Feedback, especially face-to-face, is an effective tool, if we take the time not just to hear, but to listen.

Make Your Mark

When you're at the very top of the social pyramid—
ruling a kingdom—perhaps it might seem as if
there would be no room for ambition. After all, you have
the best of everything and the power to do just about
anything you might like with it. It could be the perfect
time to rest on your laurels and let the world go by. But
a truly great ruler is one who is concerned with their legacy. As Machiavelli says, "Nothing makes a Prince so well
thought of as to undertake great enterprises and give
striking proofs of his capacity."[30]

The great stone castles dotting Europe remain tan-
gible monuments to the kings who had them built and
to the circumstances of their reigns. Unlike static monuments, castles had an immediate practical purpose
within the lifetime of these kings: to protect and defend
their families and their people and to intimidate anyone who might oppose them. William the Conqueror
set to work building castles in the immediate aftermath
of his conquest, some of which, like the White Tower
in the Tower of London and Windsor Castle, continued to be used as both seats of government and centers
of defense well into the modern day, the Tower of London housing both supplies and spies during World War
II.[31] While tourists visiting Windsor Castle may often
imagine the contemporary royals behind its walls, it
remains a symbol of the enduring power of the monarchy in England, stretching back well over a thousand
years and into the future.

Besides castle-building, another way rulers could signal the unbroken succession of their line and demonstrate

its long roots and bright future, was by giving their children symbolic names. Though it presents a nightmare for history students, styling an heir after yourself ensured that your name lived on in a literal sense, although you could also choose to hearken back to other important people from the past.[32] Edward I, for example, was the first English king baptized Edward in two centuries, but his name was an important throwback to early kings and his father's (Henry III) favorite saint. Naming his son after an esteemed pre-Conquest figure was likely particularly meaningful to Henry, who had had the phrase "ancient customs" thrown in his face his entire life, thanks to his own father and the Magna Carta.

With such a heavy weight placed on his name, perhaps it's unsurprising that Edward I was invested in creating an impressive legacy, expanding his territory to absorb Wales and fighting to conquer Scotland, too, at the time of his death. In addition to the extensive castle-building he undertook to subjugate Wales, Edward also made a show of reburying the remains of King Arthur that had been "discovered" at Glastonbury Abbey.[33] While paying tribute to this legendary ancestor, Edward was also emphasizing through burial that the "once and future king" would never return to liberate Wales. The only king they were to know, from then on, was Edward. While several monarchs named their princes Arthur, none of them ever attained the English throne, instead dying young of disease or even murder, as in the case of King John's nephew. Eventually, Arthur came to be seen as an unlucky name and has been relegated safely to middle-name status for generations.

Centuries earlier, across the Channel in France, Charlemagne had worked hard to earn his moniker—a contraction of the Latin for "Charles the Great"—and undertook many grand projects to enhance his realm.

*For medieval people, death
was never far away. Living
well ensured that a person's
reputation survived.*
Hours of René d'Anjou,
fol. 53r, c. 1410
British Library, London; Egerton 1070

These included massive efforts to improve and standard-
ize everything from weights and measures to currency
and even monastic rules. He insisted on ideas being written down, copied, and circulated among his subjects and
encouraged the development of a new way of writing.
Not content to be a forgotten ruler, he took his subjects'
welfare, body and soul, to heart, gathering the best and
brightest to his capital at Aachen, where he could hear
their ideas and implement those that he thought would
better his empire over the long run. Charlemagne's tire-
less efforts to expand and enrich his empire earned him
a name he could be proud of, perhaps allowing him to
breathe a sigh of relief at escaping the fate of his father,
Pepin the Short.

No matter what their efforts were in life, or the thinking behind them, each monarch was remembered by what
they accomplished—or didn't. Because of their repetitive
naming conventions, this might be even more true than it
is for ordinary people today. When everyone has the same
name, people find themselves leaning on things like: "Is

that the one who founded the University of Paris?" (Philip II Augustus) "Is that the one who won at Agincourt?" (Henry V) Or maybe: "Is that the one who face-planted on the beach?" (Both William I and Edward III)

Whatever we're doing—whether it's ruling a kingdom or just making our way through life—it's important to take a moment to consider what we want to be remembered for. Is it being a generous friend? A selfless volunteer? A trendsetter? A high achiever? Whatever code we live by, our actions speak louder than our words, and they will be how people remember us long after we're gone.

For a chivalrous knight, living well meant being both charitable and courageous. At the end of his life, he hoped to reach heaven as a result of his good works.
Arthurian Romances, fol. 39v, c. 1290–1300 (detail)
Yale University Library, New Haven, CT; Beineke 229

HOW TO SUCCEED IN ANY ERA

You should love loyally and live joyfully and act honorably and in good hope.
      —Geoffroi de Charny, *The Book of Chivalry*

Over the course of this book, it's probably become clear that medieval Europe constitutes a time and a place both intensely familiar and foreign to us. Many of their rules about courtesy and chivalry are entirely context-specific and often very outdated in a world where our roles and identities are (thankfully) becoming much less rigidly defined.

Words, like the societies they come from, have a way of shifting and changing over time. The phrase *common courtesy* would have been an oxymoron in a time when commoners were in the minority at court and decidedly not viewed as examples to imitate. Yet we still have courtesy in a world with few courtiers, and chivalry is often thrown around by those who have never ridden a horse, let alone put their bodies to the hazard in defense of the downtrodden.

Tradition can sometimes be used as a hiding place for those who want to close the gates against change, but while traditions are endlessly fascinating in themselves, they're not worth holding on to at the expense of other people. For some, change may be an unwelcome guest, but the truth is, it is ever at our door.

When we realize that courtesy and chivalry were always meant to keep out those who didn't belong at court or couldn't afford a horse—and when we understand that the vast majority of our ancestors wouldn't have met those conditions—it becomes clear that adhering to medieval ideas can only take us so far. Living in the modern world, we have the great benefit of hindsight, which allows us to see how outdated rules can get in the way of a fair and equal society. With that knowledge, we have the power and the responsibility to decide which ideas should remain firmly in the past.

If we strip the rules of both courtesy and chivalry back to their bare conceptual bones, they become simple: Show respect, and you will be respected. Have the courage to be both steadfast and merciful, and you will inspire people to have the courage to stand with you.

No matter which fork you use, how you dress, how much land you own, or if you've never seen a horse in your life, the only rule that really matters in the end is the golden one: treat others the way you'd wish to be treated, and your life in any era will be a better one.

Acknowledgments

I n this, as in all my projects, I continue to be grateful to all the people who have supported me through thick and thin in this most unlikely career, but courtesy dictates I should thank them yet again—something I am always most happy to do.

I owe a big and important debt of gratitude to the team at Abbeville Press who continue to believe I have a unique voice and something worth using it for. Thanks especially to Lauren Orthey, who just keeps coming up with brilliant and fun concepts, and Colette Laroya, who gives her all to ensure my books find good homes. Thanks also to Ashley Benning, who heroically wrestled with my quirky prose to better this particular book.

Endless thanks to the countless medieval scholars who have supported my career, whether through sharing their work with me on *The Medieval Podcast*, pointing me in the direction of resources, lending a kind ear, or giving me words of encouragement. The enthusiasm, joy, and generosity of the people in this community never cease to amaze me, and I feel lucky every day to work with and among you.

Helen Castor and Dan Jones, thanks for giving me warm support and encouraging kicks when I need them. I'm forever grateful for your friendship.

Thank you to Peter, Suzie, Mitch, and Emily, who valued my work enough to let me ignore them for weeks so I could write, and who have been some of my most enthusiastic cheerleaders for many years. Thank you for believing in me so effortlessly, especially when I don't believe in myself. Thanks also to Dan, who always says yes no matter what the question is. We still make a pretty awesome team, if you ask me.

Thank you to my parents, who taught me my manners as well as my letters, both of which have come in pretty handy over the years. Thanks to my brothers, who I'm endlessly proud of, and my sisters-in-law, who are just as heroic in my eyes. Thanks also to my nieces and nephews, ever-ready to ambush me with an ego boost when I least expect it, and my extended family, who never fails to support me no matter what color my hair.

I'm grateful every moment for my incredible daughters, who seem to think I can do anything. The feeling is very much mutual.

Finally, I am eternally grateful to my readers, listeners, followers, and viewers. Many of you have been along for the ride with me for years, and words can't express what an absolute privilege it is to be part of your lives. I hope this book has brought you some of the happiness that you have brought me.

Notes

INTRODUCTION

1. Daniel of Beccles, *The Book of the Civilised Man: An English Translation of the* Urbanus Magnus *of Daniel of Beccles*, trans. Fiona Whelan, Olivia Spenser, and Francesca Petrizzo (Abington, UK: Routledge, 2019), ll.13–15.

2. In medieval thinking, there were only two genders, and while a spectrum of gender identity is recognized today, modern ideas of chivalry still tend to imply a gender binary. Medieval examples in this book will follow medieval ideas of gender; however, in the modern world, it's important to be mindful of—and kind toward—people of all genders.

I
HOW TO EAT

1. Daniel of Beccles, *Book of the Civilised Man*, l.1398.

2. Daniel of Beccles, *Book of the Civilised Man*, ll.1449–50.

3. Daniel of Beccles, *Book of the Civilised Man*, l.1080.

4. *The Book of Curtasye: An English Poem of the Fourteenth Century,* trans. James Orchard Halliwell (London: C. Richards, 1841), l.115; *The Good Wife's Guide (Le Ménagier de Paris): A Medieval Household Book*, trans. Gina L. Greco and Christine M. Rose (Ithaca, NY: Cornell University Press, 2009), 270. Like today's catered events, large feasts also involved the temporary hiring of additional staff to prepare, serve, and clean up.

5. *Good Wife's Guide*, 265.

6. *Good Wife's Guide*, 268. The Goodman of Paris specifies "footed hanaps" (263) were provided for one dinner for very influential Parisians, presumably because not all hanaps were stemmed or lidded.

7. *Good Wife's Guide*, 267.

8. Daniel of Beccles, *Book of the Civilised Man*, ll.2598–99.

9. *Good Wife's Guide*, 268.

10. Rebecca Barnhouse, *The Book of the Knight of the Tower: Manners for Young Medieval Women* (New York: Palgrave Macmillan, 2006), 107.

11. *Good Wife's Guide*, 267–68.

12. Daniel of Beccles, *Book of the Civilised Man*, l.2557.

13. *Book of Curtasye*, l.343.

14. Daniel of Beccles, *Book of the Civilised Man*, l.2553.

15. Daniel of Beccles, *Book of the Civilised Man*, ll.1040, 1042.

16. Daniel of Beccles, *Book of the Civilised Man*, l.1039.

17. Roberta Gilchrist, *Medieval Life: Archaeology and the Life Course* (Woodbridge, UK: Boydell Press, 2012), 125, 144.

18. Daniel of Beccles, *Book of the Civilised Man*, ll.998–1006.

19. Daniel of Beccles, *Book of the Civilised Man*, ll.1043–45.

20. Because most medieval Europeans didn't use forks for eating, rules for their use at table aren't often recorded. It's likely they resembled those set out for spoons. Forks were instead used for cooking and serving.

21. *Book of Curtasye*, ll. 110–13; Daniel of Beccles, *Book of the Civilised Man*, ll.2615–16. The future King Edward II is shown in *Outlaw King* to eat directly off his knife, something that a prince would definitely not have done in public, even in an army camp.

22. Daniel of Beccles, *Book of the Civilised Man*, ll.931, 2577. Salt was relatively precious, but to put it back in the cellar would make a host appear petty and cheap. Daniel proposes a compromise: "Servants should not put salt that has been spilled / or has touched food back into the cellar in front of guests" (ll.2580–81).

23. Daniel of Beccles, *Book of the Civilised Man*, ll.938–40.

24. Daniel of Beccles, *Book of the Civilised Man*, ll.934, 997.

25. Ilana Krug, "*Sotelties* and Politics: The Message Behind the Food in Late Medieval Feasts" (presentation, International Congress on Medieval Studies, Kalamazoo, MI, Friday, May 11, 2018).

26. Daniel of Beccles, *Book of the Civilised Man*, ll.976–78.

27. Andreas Capellanus bluntly declares, "every woman is a drunkard." Andreas Capellanus, *The Art of Courtly Love*, trans. John Jay Parry (New York: Columbia University Press, 1941), 207.

28. Daniel of Beccles, *Book of the Civilised Man*, l.985.

29. Daniel of Beccles, *Book of the Civilised Man*, ll.1047–53.

30. Daniel of Beccles, *Book of the Civilised Man*, l.1057.

31. Daniel of Beccles, *Book of the Civilised Man*, ll.1098–1104.

32. Daniel of Beccles, *Book of the Civilised Man*, l.1049.

33. Daniel of Beccles, *Book of the Civilised Man*, ll.1312–14.

34. Daniel of Beccles, *Book of the Civilised Man*, ll.1211–14.

35. *Book of Curtasye*, ll.93–94; Daniel of Beccles, *Book of the Civilised Man*, ll.1018–19.

36. Daniel of Beccles, *Book of the Civilised Man*, ll.945–48.

II
HOW TO WOO

1. Capellanus, *Art of Courtly Love*, 28, 32–33. For Capellanus, sight is so fundamental that he claims a blind man cannot truly love unless he saw his beloved before losing his vision. The concept of love entering the heart through the eyes was so deeply entrenched in medieval thought that monks and nuns were instructed not to look, lest they were tempted. Seeing was the first step down the sinful path of lust.

2. *Carmina Burana*, vol. I, ed. and trans. David A. Traill (Cambridge, MA: Harvard University Press, 2018), 321.

3. *Carmina Burana*, vol. II, 57.

4. *The Chivalric Biography of Boucicaut Jean Il Le Meingre*, trans. Craig Taylor and Jane M. H. Taylor (Woodbridge, UK: The Boydell Press, 2016), 187.

5. Carlota Batres and Victor Shiramizu found that "across all 11 world regions [45 countries], male and female faces rated as more attractive were rated as more confident, emotionally stable, intelligent, responsible, sociable, and trustworthy." "Examining the 'Attractiveness Halo Effect' Across Cultures," *Current Psychology* (2022): 1, https://doi.org/10.1007/s12144-022-03575-0. Fortunately, M. Luisa Demattè, Robert

Österbauer, and Charles Spence found that something as simple as smelling good can boost attractiveness. "Olfactory Cues Modulate Facial Attractiveness," *Chemical Senses* 32, no. 6 (2007): 1, https://doi.org/10.1093/chemse/bjm030, 603–10.

6. Daniel of Beccles, *Book of the Civilised Man*, ll.1180–90.

7. Barnhouse, *Book of the Knight of the Tower*, 126–28.

8. Barnhouse, *Book of the Knight of the Tower*, 72.

9. Barnhouse, *Book of the Knight of the Tower*, 124. Another medieval manual, *The Mirror for Good Women*, blames the lust inflamed by women's cosmetics and fashion as the cause of the great flood in Genesis.

10. Many of these can be found in *The Trotula*, a compendium of medical advice for women, which we'll look at again in chapter four. See Monica Green, ed., *The Trotula, An English Translation of the Medieval Compendium of Women's Medicine* (Philadelphia: University of Pennsylvania Press, 2002).

11. Barnhouse, *Book of the Knight of the Tower*, 82, 84.

12. Barnhouse, *Book of the Knight of the Tower*, 130.

13. David Green. *The Hundred Years War: A People's History* (New Haven, CT: Yale University Press, 2014), 193.

14. Barnhouse, *Book of the Knight of the Tower*, 122.

15. Capellanus, *Art of Courtly Love*, 176. It's unlikely that this is an actual quote from the countess, but rather an imagined version voiced by the author.

16. Roberta Gilchrist, *Medieval Life: Archaeology and the Life Course* (Rochester, NY: Boydell & Brewer, 2012), 74–57, 94; and Janet S. Loengard, " 'Which May be Said to be her Own': Widows and Goods in Late-Medieval England," in *Medieval Domesticity: Home, Housing and Household in Medieval England*, eds. Maryanne Kowaleski and P. J. P. Goldberg (Cambridge, UK: Cambridge University Press, 2008), 167, who writes, "for most women, their girdles were their most precious possessions."

17. David Crouch, *Tournament* (London: Hambledon and Continuum, 2006), 139, 159. Men also wore love tokens into battle. A spur found at the battle site at Towton says, "You have all my heart with love." Society of Antiquaries of London, "Medieval spur from the site of the Battle of Towton," accessed September 30, 2022, https://www.sal.org.uk/

collections/explore-our-collections/collections-highlights/
medieval-spur-from-the-site-of-the-battle-of-towton.

18. Daniel of Beccles, *Book of the Civilised Man*, l.103.

19. Barnhouse, *Book of the Knight of the Tower*, 79.

20. Daniel of Beccles, *Book of the Civilised Man*, ll.881–84.

21. Daniel of Beccles, *Book of the Civilised Man*, ll.1456, 884. Many people, especially women, still politely cover their mouths when they laugh.

22. Capellanus, *Art of Courtly Love*, 185. Capellanus also says that beautiful people may fall in love easily, but their relationships don't last because they lack the wisdom to be discreet (34–35). The false dichotomy of beauty versus brains is one of many problematic elements of courtly love that has outlasted the Middle Ages.

23. Capellanus, *Art of Courtly Love*, 185, 199, 158.

24. Peter Konieczny, "How to Tell If a Woman Is In Love with You—Medieval Edition," Medievalists.net, July 2022, https://www.medievalists.net/2022/07/how-to-tell-if-a-woman-is-in-love-with-you-medieval-edition; Capellanus, *Art of Courtly Love*, 199.

25. Internationally renowned body language expert Joe Navarro confirms that grooming behaviors and frequent glances can be positive signs of interest, although lip biting is not. When it comes to nonverbal communication, it's important to take more than one signal into account. For Navarro's quick over-view of flirtatious behavior, see "A Body Language Expert Explains How to Tell If a Woman is Actually Into You," *Men's Health*, September 18, 2019, https://www.menshealth.com/sex-women/a29105484/mixed-signals.

26. Daniel of Beccles, *Book of the Civilised Man*, ll.1457, 1461.

27. Daniel of Beccles, *Book of the Civilised Man*, ll.664–67, 889. To call upon God was to bring him into your presence, which wasn't to be done lightly, especially since this meant you could be prodding Jesus's wounds by summoning them. God's name was invoked to ask him to witness or do something (such as literally damning people), which is why using taboo words today is still called "swearing," "cursing," or speaking "oaths." Over time, people became more prudish about bodies than blasphemy, and swearing shifted to encompass words about bodily functions or acts. Remnants of medieval swearing can still be found

in the comic book word *zounds*, a contraction of "God's/Christ's wounds."

28. *The History of William Marshal: The True Story of England's Greatest Knight*, trans. Nigel Bryant (Woodbridge, UK: Boydell & Brewer, 2016), 165. Other popular exclamations are "God's eyes" (106) and "God's legs" (125).

29. Barnhouse, *Book of the Knight of the Tower*, 81.

30. Ibid.

31. Consent is a complex issue when it comes to medieval love and sex. A marriage that was known to be coerced was not binding, but there were many circumstances in which people might outwardly agree to a marriage they did not want. Consent was essential in sexual encounters, and rape was always a crime; however, spouses owed a "marital debt" to their partners, which meant that marital rape was a contradiction in terms. It was also an accepted part of medieval culture that women were to be coquettish and their resistance—even if it involved tears—was a formality to be overcome. Sadly, these attitudes have only very recently been challenged on a broad scale and persist in many instances, as the #metoo movement has shown.

32. Of course, the murders of the Princes in the Tower also cleared the way for Richard. Edward and Elizabeth did have an important witness at their wedding—her mother, Jacquetta Woodville—but given Jacquetta's investment in the marriage, her testimony was considered suspect. Gemma Hollman, *Royal Witches* (Cheltenham, UK: The History Press, 2019), 210.

33. Helen Castor, *Blood and Roses: One Family's Struggle and Triumph During the Tumultuous Wars of the Roses* (New York: Harper Perennial, 2006), 269–70.

34. The idea of love as suffering predates the Middle Ages, but it was eagerly adopted by the songwriters of the twelfth century.

35. William D. Paden and Frances Freeman Paden, *Troubadour Poems from the South of France* (Cambridge, UK: D. S. Brewer, 2007), 38.

36. It is a myth that medieval people never traveled anywhere. They journeyed for a myriad of reasons; trade, war, and pilgrimage being just a few.

37. "Anonymous Letter Between Two Twelfth-Century Nuns," trans. Peter Dronke, in *Handbook of Medieval Sexuality*, ed. Vern

L. Bullough and James A. Brundage (New York: Routledge, 2010), 211.

38. Paden and Paden, *Troubadour Poems from the South of France*, 83.

III
HOW TO FIGHT

1. Ramon Llull, *The Book of the Order of Chivalry*, trans. Noel Fallows (Woodbridge, UK: The Boydell Press, 2013), 42.

2. *History of William Marshal*, 35.

3. Llull, *Book of the Order of Chivalry*, 56, 42.

4. *History of William Marshal*, 50.

5. Anastasija Ropa and Timothy Dawson, "Medieval Horses with Anastasija Ropa and Timothy Dawson," *The Medieval Podcast*, produced by Danièle Cybulskie, July 13, 2022, https://www.medievalists.net/2022/07/medieval-horses-with-anastasija-ropa-and-timothy-dawson/.

6. *History of William Marshal*, 80.

7. Publius Flavius Vegetius Renatus, *Vegetius: The Epitome of Military Science*, 2nd ed., trans. N. P. Milner (Liverpool, UK: Liverpool University Press, 2001), 57.

8. Unlike soldiers in a standing army, who live and work together in times of both war and peace, knights were summoned only when needed.

9. Vegetius, 58.

10. *Chivalric Biography of Boucicaut*, 30–31. For a video demonstration of Boucicaut's training using reconstructed armor, see Daniel Jaquet, "Can You Move in Armour?" Medievalists.net YouTube Channel, July 1, 2016, https://youtu.be/q-bnM5SuQkI.

11. *History of William Marshal*, 63.

12. Richard W. Kaeuper and Elspeth Kennedy, The Book of Chivalry *of Geoffroi de Charny: Text, Context, and Translation* (Philadelphia: University of Pennsylvania Press, 1996), 169–71. It is Kaeuper and Kennedy who suggest that the collee given to the squire is "a light tap, probably here with a sword," while Llull (*Book of the Order of Chivalry*) is explicit that this is a "hard slap" (65). Llull was writing in thirteenth-century Catalonia, while Charny was writing in fourteenth-century France.

13. Llull, *Book of the Order of Chivalry*, 65.

14. Kaeuper and Kennedy, Book of Chivalry *of Geoffroi de Charny*, 101.

15. Eric Jager, *The Last Duel* (New York: Broadway Books, 2004), 146.

16. *History of William Marshal*, 78.

17. *History of William Marshal*, 59.

18. *Vegetius*, 86.

19. *Vegetius*, 59.

20. Kaeuper and Kennedy, Book of Chivalry *of Geoffroi de Charny*, 165.

21. *Vegetius*, 92.

22. *History of William Marshal*, 37.

23. In addition to being a symbol of the divine, Joan inspired the French army by fighting while injured and ensuring she was on the front lines. Kelly DeVries, *Joan of Arc: A Military Leader* (Phoenix Mill, UK: Sutton Publishing, 1999), 101.

24. *Chivalric Biography of Boucicaut*, 201–2. In Capellanus's *The Art of Courtly Love*, a noblewoman declares, "We think that a woman is unworthy of any honor if she has decided that her lover ought to be deprived of her love because of some deformity resulting from the common chance of war, which is apt to happen to those who fight bravely" (174), lending further reassurance to knights departing for war.

25. Vegetius writes this as a warning against accidentally inspiring such desperate courage in the enemy. Instead, a leader should deliberately create an opening for flight. "For when an escape-route is revealed, the minds of all are united on turning their backs, and they are slaughtered unavenged, like cattle" (107).

26. Kaeuper and Kennedy, Book of Chivalry *of Geoffroi de Charny*, 131.

27. Kaeuper and Kennedy, Book of Chivalry *of Geoffroi de Charny*, 131.

28. Thomas Malory, *Le Morte Darthur*, ed. Stephen H. A. Shepherd (New York: W. W. Norton, 2004), 68–70.

29. While the Company of the Star no longer exists, the Order of the Garter survives today, boasting King Charles III and Prince William as members.

30. Jean de Bueil, *Jean de Bueil: Le Jouvencel*, trans. Craig Taylor and Jane M. H. Taylor (Woodbridge, UK: The Boydell Press, 2020), 35.

31. Llull, *Book of the Order of Chivalry*, 50.

32. Kaeuper and Kennedy, Book of Chivalry *of Geoffroi de Charny*, 131.

33. *Chivalric Biography of Boucicaut*, 90–91.

34. Llull, *Book of the Order of Chivalry*, 41.

35. In *The Art of Courtly Love*, Capellanus says, "When a woman has granted any man the hope of her love … and she finds him not unworthy of this love, it is very wrong for her to try to deprive him of the love he has so long hoped for" (166).

IV
HOW TO RUN A HOUSEHOLD

1. Green, *Trotula*, 76–78.

2. It's not completely clear as to whether or not the advice in *The Distaff Gospels* is real or satire, given the overall tone of the text. My suspicion is that both real and satirical advice is mixed up within *The Distaff Gospels*, although it's impossible to tell which is which. Madeline Jeay and Kathleen Garay, eds. *The Distaff Gospels* (Peterborough, ON: Broadview Press, 2006).

3. Jeay and Garay, *Distaff Gospels*, 171.

4. Green, Trotula, 77. Both *The Trotula* and *The Distaff Gospels* warn against tempting women with anything they can't eat, in case of miscarriage or birthmarks, respectively (77, 95). *The Distaff Gospels* also contain dire warnings against eating hares or fish heads in case they affect the development of the child's mouth (87, 97).

5. Jeay and Garay, *Distaff Gospels*, 85.

6. Green, *Trotula*, 81.

7. Nicholas Orme, *Medieval Children* (New Haven, CT: Yale University Press, 2003), 35, 37. It's extremely unlikely all these children survived infancy, meaning that, in the end, the family likely only had one child with each name.

8. Orme, *Medieval Children*, 59, 63.

9. Jeay and Garay, *Distaff Gospels*, 93; Orme, *Medieval Children*, 64.

10. Orme, *Medieval Children*, 58.

11. Orme, *Medieval Children*, 167; Gilchrist, *Medieval Life*, 143.

12. Orme, *Medieval Children*, 167–72.

13. Christine de Pizan, *The Selected Writings of Christine de Pizan*, trans. Renate Blumenfeld-Kosinski and Kevin Brownlee, ed. Renate Blumenfeld-Kosinski (New York: W. W. Norton, 1997), 192.

14. Daniel of Beccles, *Book of the Civilised Man*, ll.1722–27.

15. Orme, *Medieval Children*, 307.

16. Orme, *Medieval Children*, 243–45.

17. Barnhouse, *Book of the Knight of the Tower*, 111.

18. Lady Reason goes on to say that women "know less" because they stay at home and don't experience as much of the world, not because they're intellectually inferior. Christine de Pizan, The Book of the City of Ladies *and Other Writings*, ed. Sophie Bourgault and Rebecca Kingston (Indianapolis: Hackett Publishing, 2018), 68–69.

19. Pizan, *Selected Writings*, 204.

20. Orme, *Medieval Children*, 56; Barnhouse, *Book of the Knight of the Tower*, 112.

21. Orme, *Medieval Children*, 334–37.

22. Orme, *Medieval Children*, 315–16.

23. Pizan, *Selected Writings*, 167.

24. "How the Goode Wife Taught Hyr Doughter," in *The Trials and Joys of Marriage*, ed. Eve Salisbury (Kalamazoo, MI: Medieval Institute Publications, 2002), ll.181–83; *Good Wife's Guide*, 223.

25. It goes without saying that part of this protection involved preventing the unwanted attentions of men, a very real danger to young women, especially servants.

26. Unmarried men left such important work to their mothers, but for simplicity, we'll stick with wives.

27. *Good Wife's Guide*, 49

28. *Good Wife's Guide*, 181.

29. Ibid.

30. "How the Goode Wife Taught Hyr Doughter," ll.153–54.

31. The Paston Letters, #88. This woman is not the same as the steadfast newlywed we met in chapter two, but another Paston matriarch. https://fiftywordsforsnow.com/ebooks/paston/paston2.html.

32. *Good Wife's Guide*, 181. While spices weren't scarce in medieval Europe, some of them could be quite pricey. This is just one of the reasons why the old idea that people spiced their food to disguise its rottenness is a myth. It would be a waste of money to spice bad food in addition to it being risky—possibly fatal—to eat it.

33. *Good Wife's Guide*, 268.

34. Orme, *Medieval Children*, 19–21.

35. In one touching early modern will that attests to the serious organization of some women, a mother (Alice Lord) bequeathed bedding to each of her sons, noting that she had already packaged up the sets and written their names on each bundle. Katherine French found in her survey of post-plague wills that "women specified twice as often as men the room in which an object could be found," which demonstrates their intimate knowledge of their households and their possessions. Katherine French, *Household Goods and Good Households in Late Medieval London: Consumption and Domesticity after the Plague* (Philadelphia: University of Pennsylvania Press, 2021), 125, 121.

36. *Good Wife's Guide*, 220.

37. *Good Wife's Guide*, 222–23, 219.

38. *Good Wife's Guide*, 183.

39. *Chivalric Biography of Boucicaut*, 204. Boucicaut, who was governing a city at the time, had more responsibilities than the average rural lord; however, the structure of his days is similar.

40. Niccolò Machiavelli, *The Prince*, trans. N. H. Thompson (New York: Dover Publications), 25.

41. Machiavelli, *Prince*, 19.

42. *Good Wife's Guide*, 141, 131.

43. *Good Wife's Guide*, 138.

44. *Good Wife's Guide*, 130, 137.

45. *Good Wife's Guide,* 174–76.

46. Pizan, *Selected Writings*, 167–68.

47. For Lucy's remarkable life, see Bridget Wells-Furby, *Aristocratic Marriage, Adultery and Divorce in the Fourteenth Century: The Life of Lucy de Thweng* (Woodbridge, UK: Boydell, 2019).

48. "How the Goode Man Taght Hys Sone," in Salisbury, *Trials and Joys of Marriage*, ll.89–100.

49. This is said to be the "oldest surviving Valentine's letter in the English language," penned by yet another Paston bride, with another husband named John. British Library, "Valentine's Day Love Letter, February 1477," accessed September 30, 2022, https://www.bl.uk/learning/timeline/item126579.html.

50. "How the Goode Man Taght Hys Sone," ll.130–36. Medieval husbands did have the legal right to "discipline" their wives physically; however, many treatises criticize this as being counterproductive. Unsurprisingly, they say that beatings make women resentful, and they won't behave better because of them.

51. Capellanus, *Art of Courtly Love*, 175.

52. Pizan, *Selected Writings*, 101–2.

53. Though it appears Edward loved Elizabeth steadfastly, and in the face of strong opposition, it didn't stop him from being the king who had the most affairs of anyone in this list.

V
HOW TO RULE A KINGDOM

1. Although divorce was prohibited by the medieval church, couples who were incompatible or childless could petition the pope for an annulment. Louis and Eleanor's annulment was granted citing consanguinity: being too closely related. While the dissolution of their marriage should have rendered their daughters illegitimate, the couple's high status allowed for the rules to be bent. Eleanor was free to marry Henry; Louis was free to marry a new queen who could bear him a male heir; and their daughters retained their titles. Their eldest, Marie de Champagne, was Andreas Capellanus's alleged authority on courtly love.

2. Boucicaut, who we've encountered many times in this book, was one of the few held for ransom after Agincourt. As marshal of France, he was a very important prisoner, indeed. In the end, no one could agree on the terms for his ransom, and he died in England six years later. *Chivalric Biography of Boucicaut*, 6–7.

3. Machiavelli, *Prince*, 10.

4. Machiavelli, *Prince*, 11.

5. Machiavelli, *Prince*, 40.

6. Philip Augustus's biographer said the French king was sent to be "a bit in [Henry's] mouth, to vindicate the blood of the blessed martyr Thomas of Canterbury, so that through grief He might give him understanding and return him to the bosom of the mother church." Rigord, *The Deeds of Philip Augustus: An English Translation of Rigord's* Gest Philippi Augusti, trans. Larry Field, ed. M. Cecilia Gaposchkin and Sean L. Field (Ithaca, NY: Cornell University Press, 2022), 111.

7. He cedes that some missions should be private, but points out that "no two powers [i.e., kingdoms] can confront each other without this becoming general knowledge." *Jean de Bueil*, 232, 235.

8. Machiavelli, *Prince*, 40.

9. Machiavelli, *Prince*, 41.

10. Benedict of Nursia, *The Rule of St. Benedict*, trans. Bruce L. Venarde (Cambridge, MA: Harvard University Press, 2011), 173.

11. Rigord, *Deeds of Philip Augustus*, 123.

12. Sarah Fiddyment, Natalie J. Goodison, Elma Brenner, Stefania Signorello, Kierri Price, and Matthew J. Collins, "Girding the Loins? Direct Evidence of the Use of a Medieval English Parchment Birthing Girdle from Biomolecular Analysis," *Royal Society Open Science*, March 10, 2021, https://doi.org/10.1098/rsos.202055; Jack Hartnell, *Medieval Bodies: Life and Death in the Middle Ages* (New York: W. W. Norton, 2018), 75. As Jack Hartnell says, "The mouth was a key point for the sacred to flow back and forth."

13. Jean Froissart, *Chronicles*, trans. Geoffrey Brereton (New York: Penguin, 1968), 327.

14. Kiril Petkov called the kiss of peace "the most powerful peace act," since it "brought about the fulfillment of the most perfect condition, the 'Peace of Jerusalem,' through which God reconciled humankind . . . freeing the heart of worldly hatred." *The Kiss of Peace: Ritual, Self, and Society in the High and Late Medieval West* (Leiden, the Netherlands: Brill, 2003), 2–3.

15. Froissart, *Chronicles*, 327.

16. Daniel of Beccles, *Book of the Civilised Man*, ll.1416–18.

17. Pizan, *Selected Writings*, 163.

18. Pizan, *Selected Writings*, 164.

19. Philippa is said to have given the burghers clothes, "an ample dinner," and safe passage (Froissart, *Chronicles*, 109). Gemma Hollman has shown that Philippa was not actually pregnant at this time. Medieval chroniclers are known for embroidering the truth, and this is a conventional embellishment to make the moment more poignant. *The Queen and the Mistress: The Women of Edward II* (Cheltenham, UK: The History Press, 2022), 81.

20. Machiavelli, *Prince*, 32.

21. D. A. Carpenter, *The Reign of Henry III* (London: The Hambledon Press, 2006), 436. Richard was imprisoned by the Holy Roman Emperor on his journey home from the Middle East. His ransom has become a central part of the Robin Hood legend in the centuries since.

22. Michael Burger, ed. *Sources for the History of Western Civilization, Volume 1* (Toronto: University of Toronto Press, 2015), 386–87.

23. Rigord, *Deeds of Philip Augustus*, 93.

24. Machiavelli, *Prince*, 27, 39. He says "credit" because he believed that while a person should seem generous, they should not be so generous that they have to tax people to fund this generosity, or goodwill will quickly evaporate. It's the appearance of largesse that matters.

25. Rigord, *Deeds of Philip Augustus*, 79.

26. *Jean de Bueil*, 143.

27. Machiavelli, *Prince*, 18.

28. Machiavelli, *Prince*, 30.

29. Although it's often revered as a gesture toward equality and even democracy, the Magna Carta is almost exclusively concerned with baronial rights, not the rights of the peasantry or unfree serfs.

30. Machiavelli, *Prince*, 38.

31. These spies were Germans, held prisoner and executed there. Historic Royal Palaces, "The Tower at War," accessed October 29, 2022, https://www.hrp.org.uk/tower-of-london/history-and-stories/the-tower-at-war/#gs.h6kf1f.

32. The current English king, Charles III, caused a small stir among
    royalists when he chose this as his regnal name
    because of the weight of history behind it. The previous two
    kings named Charles had complicated reigns to say the least,
    with Charles I losing his head to Oliver Cromwell and Charles
    II spending years of his reign in exile. Should Prince William,
    in turn, choose to keep his own name as his regnal name, it
    should raise fewer eyebrows.

33. Marc Morris, *A Great and Terrible King: Edward I and the Forging
    of Britain* (London: Windmill Books, 2009), 72.

Recommended Reading

"Anonymous Letter Between Two Twelfth-Century Nuns," translated by Peter Dronke. In *Handbook of Medieval Sexuality*, edited by Vern L. Bullough and James A. Brundage, 211. New York: Routledge, 2010.

Barnhouse, Rebecca. *The Book of the Knight of the Tower: Manners for Young Medieval Women*. New York: Palgrave Macmillan, 2006.

Batres, Carlota, and Victor Shiramizu. "Examining the 'Attractiveness Halo Effect' Across Cultures." *Current Psychology* (2022). https://doi.org/10.1007/s12144-022-03575-0.

Benedict of Nursia. *The Rule of St. Benedict*. Translated by Bruce L. Venarde. Cambridge, MA: Harvard University Press, 2011.

The Book of Curtasye: An English Poem of the Fourteenth Century. Translated by James Orchard Halliwell. London: C. Richards, 1841.

British Library. "Valentine's Day Love Letter, February 1477." Accessed September 30, 2022. https://www.bl.uk/learning/timeline/item126579.html. October 11, 2022.

Burger, Michael, ed. *Sources for the History of Western Civilization*, vol I. Toronto: University of Toronto Press, 2015.

Capellanus, Andreas. *The Art of Courtly Love*. Translated by John Jay Parry. New York: Columbia University Press, 1941.

Carmina Burana, vols. I and II. Edited and translated by David A. Traill. Cambridge, MA: Harvard University Press, 2018.

Carpenter, D. A. *The Reign of Henry III*. London: The Hambledon Press, 2006.

Castor, Helen. *Blood and Roses: One Family's Struggle and Triumph During the Tumultuous Wars of the Roses*. New York: Harper Perennial, 2006.

The Chivalric Biography of Boucicaut Jean II Le Meingre. Translated by Craig Taylor and Jane M. H. Taylor. Woodbridge, UK: The Boydell Press, 2016.

Crouch, David. *Tournament*. London: Hambledon and Continuum, 2006.

Daniel of Beccles. *The Book of the Civilised Man: An English Translation of the* Urbanus Magnus *of Daniel of Beccles*. Translated by Fiona

Whelan, Olivia Spenser, and Francesca Petrizzo. Abington, UK: Routledge, 2019.

De Bueil, Jean. *Jean de Bueil*: Le Jouvencel. Translated by Craig Taylor and Jane M. H. Taylor. Woodbridge, UK: The Boydell Press, 2020.

Demattè, M. Luisa, Robert Österbauer, and Charles Spence. "Olfactory Cues Modulate Facial Attractiveness." *Chemical Senses* 32, no. 6 (2007): 603–10. https://doi.org/10.1093/chemse/bjm030.

De Pizan, Christine. The Book of the City of Ladies *and Other Writings*. Edited by Sophie Bourgault and Rebecca Kingston. Indianapolis: Hackett Publishing, 2018.

———. *The Selected Writings of Christine de Pizan*. Translated by Renate Blumenfeld-Kosinski and Kevin Brownlee and edited by Renate Blumenfeld-Kosinski. New York: W. W. Norton, 1997.

DeVries, Kelly. *Joan of Arc: A Military Leader.* Phoenix Mill, UK: Sutton Publishing, 1999.

Fiddyment, Sarah, Natalie J. Goodison, Elma Brenner, Stefania Signorello, Kierri Price, and Matthew J. Collins. "Girding the Loins? Direct Evidence of the Use of a Medieval English Parchment Birthing Girdle from Biomolecular Analysis." *Royal Society Open Science*, March 10, 2021. https://doi.org/10.1098/rsos.202055.

French, Katherine L. *Household Goods and Good Households in Late Medieval London: Consumption and Domesticity after the Plague.* Philadelphia: University of Pennsylvania Press, 2021.

Froissart, Jean. *Chronicles.* Translated by Geoffrey Brereton. New York: Penguin, 1968.

Gilchrist, Roberta. *Medieval Life: Archaeology and the Life Course.* Woodbridge, UK: Boydell Press, 2012.

The Good Wife's Guide (Le Ménagier de Paris): A Medieval Household Book. Translated by Gina L. Greco and Christine M. Rose. Ithaca, NY: Cornell University Press, 2009.

Green, David. *The Hundred Years War: A People's History.* New Haven, CT: Yale University Press, 2014.

Green, Monica, ed. *The Trotula: An English Translation of the Medieval Compendium of Women's Medicine.* Philadelphia: University of Pennsylvania Press, 2002.

Hartnell, Jack. *Medieval Bodies: Life and Death in the Middle Ages.* New York: W. W. Norton, 2018.

Historic Royal Palaces. "The Tower at War." Accessed October 29, 2022. https://www.hrp.org.uk/tower-of-london/history-and-stories/the-tower-at-war/#gs.h6kf1f.

The History of William Marshal: The True Story of England's Greatest Knight. Translated by Nigel Bryant. Woodbridge, UK: Boydell & Brewer, 2016.

Hollman, Gemma. *The Queen and the Mistress: The Women of Edward II.* Cheltenham, UK: The History Press, 2022.

———. *Royal Witches.* Cheltenham, UK: The History Press, 2019.

Jager, Eric. *The Last Duel.* New York: Broadway Books, 2004.

Jaquet, Daniel. "Can You Move in Armour?" *Medievalists.net* YouTube Channel. July 1, 2016. https://www.youtube.com/watch?v=q-bnM5SuQkI.

Jeay, Madeline, and Kathleen Garay, eds. *The Distaff Gospels.* Peterborough, ON: Broadview Press, 2006.

Kaeuper, Richard W., and Elspeth Kennedy. *The Book of Chivalry of Geoffroi de Charny: Text, Context, and Translation.* Philadelphia: University of Pennsylvania Press, 1996.

Konieczny, Peter. "How to Tell if A Woman is In Love With You—Medieval Edition." Medievalists.net. July 2022. https://www.medievalists.net/2022/07/how-to-tell-if-a-woman-is-in-love-with-you-medieval-edition.

Krug, Ilana. "*Sotelties* and Politics: The Message Behind the Food in Late Medieval Feasts." Paper presented at the International Congress on Medieval Studies, Kalamazoo, MI, Friday, May 11, 2018.

Llull, Ramon. *The Book of the Order of Chivalry.* Translated by Noel Fallows. Woodbridge, UK: The Boydell Press, 2013.

Loengard, Janet S. " 'Which May Be Said to Be Her Own': Widows and Goods in Late-Medieval England." In *Medieval Domesticity: Home, Housing and Household in Medieval England*, edited by Maryanne Kowaleski and P. J. P. Goldberg. Cambridge, UK: Cambridge University Press, 2008.

Machiavelli, Niccolò. *The Prince.* Translated by N. H. Thompson. New York: Dover Publications, 1992.

Malory, Thomas. *Le Morte Darthur.* Edited by Stephen H. A. Shepherd. New York: W. W. Norton, 2004.

McDougall, Sara. "Bastard Priests: Illegitimacy and Ordination in Medieval Europe." *Speculum* 94, no. 1 (January 2019): 138–72.

Morris, Marc. *A Great and Terrible King: Edward I and the Forging of Britain*. London: Windmill Books, 2009.

Navarro, Joe. "A Body Language Expert Explains How to Tell if a Woman is Actually Into You." *Men's Health*, September 18, 2019. https://www.menshealth.com/sex-women/a29105484/mixed-signals.

Orme, Nicholas. *Medieval Children*. New Haven, CT: Yale University Press, 2003.

Paden, William D., and Frances Freeman Paden. *Troubadour Poems from the South of France*. Cambridge, UK: D. S. Brewer, 2007.

Petkov, Kiril. *The Kiss of Peace: Ritual, Self, and Society in the High and Late Medieval West*. Leiden, the Netherlands: Brill, 2003.

Phillips, Noëlle. *Craft Beer Culture and Modern Medievalism: Brewing Dissent*. Leeds, UK: Arc Humanities Press, 2020.

Rawcliffe, Carole. *Urban Bodies: Communal Health in Late Medieval English Towns and Cities*. Woodbridge, UK: The Boydell Press, 2013.

Rigord. *The Deeds of Philip Augustus: An English Translation of Rigord's Gesta Philippi Augusti*. Translated by Larry F. Field and edited by M. Cecilia Gaposchkin and Sean L. Field. Ithaca, NY: Cornell University Press, 2022.

Ropa, Anastasija, and Timothy Dawson. "Medieval Horses with Anastasija Ropa and Timothy Dawson." *The Medieval Podcast*. Produced by Danièle Cybulskie. July 13, 2022. https://www.medievalists.net/2022/07/medieval-horses-with-anastasija-ropa-and-timothy-dawson/.

Salisbury, Eve, ed. *The Trials and Joys of Marriage*. Kalamazoo, MI: Medieval Institute Publications, 2002.

Society of Antiquaries of London. "Medieval spur from the site of the Battle of Towton." Accessed September 30, 2022. https://www.sal.org.uk/collections/explore-our-collections/collections-highlights/medieval-spur-from-the-site-of-the-battle-of-towton.

Vegetius Renatus, Publius Flavius. *Vegetius: The Epitome of Military Science*. 2nd edition. Translated by N. P. Milner. Liverpool, UK: Liverpool University Press, 2001.

Wells-Furby, Bridget. *Aristocratic Marriage, Adultery and Divorce in the Fourteenth Century: The Life of Lucy de Thweng*. Woodbridge, UK: Boydell, 2019.

Index

Illustration Credits

Art Resource (Victoria and Albert Museum, London): p. 21. *British Library, London © The Granger Collection Ltd d/b/a GRANGER Historical Picture Archive*: pp. 9, 33, 39, 47, 56, 63, 65, 69, 73, 93, 113, 114, 117, 121, 131, 140, 146. *British Museum, London*: p. 21. *Getty Museum, Los Angeles*: pp. 18, 24, 25, 37, 38, 45, 50, 58, 60, 67, 75, 76, 78, 80, 88, 90, 101, 102, 104, 129, 136, 138, 143. *By courtesy of the Honourable Societies of Inner and Middle Temple, London*: p. 55. *The Met Cloisters, New York*: pp. 14, 16, 17, 19, 23, 35, 40, 41, 62, 66, 97, 108, 135. *National Archives, Washington, DC*: p. 142. *National Gallery of Art, Washington, DC*: pp. 83, 118. *Science Museum, London*: p. 28. *Walters Art Museum, Baltimore*: pp. 40, 48, 84, 87, 111. *Wikimedia Commons*: pp. 57, 59, 120, 124, 133, 137. *Yale University Library, New Haven, CT*: pp. 15, 42, 71, 91, 96, 110, 126, 139, 147